7 Seasons of Crisis and Renewal

Patrick M. Morley

LifeWay Press®
Nashville, Tennessee

To Tommy Boroughs, Chuck Green, Chuck Mitchell, and Ken Moar—
Thanks for helping me find God's grace in each of my seasons.

© 1996 • Patrick Morley
Fifth Printing 2006

No part of this book may be reproduced or transmitted in any form or by any means, electronic or mechanical, including photocopying and recording, or by any information storage or retrieval system, except as may be expressly permitted in writing by the publisher. Requests for permission should be addressed in writing to LifeWay Press®; One LifeWay Plaza; Nashville, TN 37234-0175.

ISBN 0-8054-9787-0

This book is a resource in the Personal Life subject area
of the Christian Growth Study Plan.
Course CG-0179

Dewey Decimal Classification: 248.842
Subject Heading: MEN \ RELIGIOUS LIFE

Printed in the United States of America

The Curriculum Products are based on *The Seven Seasons of a Man's Life*, by Patrick Morley, and created under license granted by Thomas Nelson, Inc.

Unless otherwise indicated, Scripture quotations are from the Holy Bible, New International Version, copyright © 1973,1978,1984, by International Bible Society.

Scripture quotations marked NKJV are from the New King James Version. Copyright © 1979, 1980, 1982, Thomas Nelson, Inc., Publishers.

Scripture quotations marked TLB are taken from The Living Bible. Copyright © Tyndale House Publishers, Wheaton, Illinois, 1971. Used by permission.

Design: Edward Crawford
Cover Illustration: Michael Schwab
Icons: CSA Archive
Curriculum Writer: Larry Keefauver
Coordinating Editor: David Delk

Leadership and Adult Publishing
LifeWay Church Resources
One LifeWay Plaza
Nashville, TN 37234-0175

CONTENTS

Introduction 4

Life's Seasons 6

The Season of Crisis

Week 1: Burnout 8
• The Symptoms in a Time of Crisis • Root Problems of Burnout • Values, What's Important? • Expectations, What's Due? • A Sense of Purpose, and Unresolved Issues

Week 2: The Dark Night of the Soul 29
• The Root Problem of Cultural Christianity • Understanding Cultural Christianity • Accepting Responsibility for the Problem • Accepting Responsibility for the Solution • The Way Back

The Season of Renewal

Week 3: Restoration 50
• Rebellion • Reversals • Repentance • Restoration • Two Lessons From the Parable

Week 4: A New Message for Men 69
• The Two-Story Kingdom • *Who* Am I? -vs- *Whose* Am I? • *What* -vs- *Who* Is the Purpose of My Life? • An Organizing Principle • The Challenge to Change Paradigms

Week 5: Defining Moments 88
• Defining Moments: What Are They? • Defining Moment 1: Control • Defining Moment 2: Character • Defining Moment 3: Confidence • Defining Moment 4: Calling

Week 6: Reflecting on Crisis and Renewal 109
• Burnout • The Dark Night of the Soul • Restoration • A New Message for Men • Defining Moments

Leader Guide 128

INTRODUCTION

WELCOME to *The Seasons of Crisis and Renewal*. Each man experiences crises when his world seems to be crashing in around him. And after these crises there is often a time of picking up the pieces, a time of renewal. I want you to know …

You are not alone. I have discovered that every man experiences seven seasons during his life.

 The Season of Reflection

 The Season of Building

 The Season of Crisis

 The Season of Renewal

 The Season of Rebuilding

 The Season of Suffering

 The Season of Success

I have prepared four books in this collection to help you explore these seasons. This book focuses on the seasons of crisis and renewal.

Each week during the next six weeks you will have five daily studies to read and complete. You will need 20 to 30 minutes each day.

Each day a BIG IDEA will be presented. The BIG IDEA (identified with this symbol ◆) captures the main point for that day's lesson in one sentence. The rest of the material for that day amplifies, expands, explains, and applies the BIG IDEA.

You will also read other statements with which you will highly identify. Let me encourage you to underline, make notes, and write down questions about ideas you don't agree with or understand. If you are studying with a group, bring up your questions with the other men.

For added review, a list of key ideas called *The Bottom Line* appears at the end of each day's lesson.

Let me urge you to find a group of men to study with you. Use the Leader Guide on pages 128-141. This investment will bring a great return.

You and your spiritual pilgrimage are the focal point of this study. The subject is God and wisdom to live under His authority and grace. So, in each lesson you will be encouraged to apply the truths and principles to your life situation.

I pray that God will use this study in a wonderful and powerful way in your life. Millions of men are experiencing a hunger for God. They want to think more deeply about their lives. They are seeking to become the spiritual leaders of their homes and discover God's will for their lives. Whichever season of life you find yourself in, this study will encourage you to keep going.

MAN IN THE MIRROR CONTACTS

Men's Events
E-mail *events@maninthemirror.org*, or call 800-929-2536 ex. 3

Resources
E-mail *resources@maninthemirror.org*, or call 800-929-2536 ex. 2.

Mass Books
E-mail *books@maninthemirror.org*, or cal 800-929-2536 ex. 126.

Donations and Small Group Partnerships
E-mail *partners@maninthemirror.org*, or call 800-929-2536 ex. 133

Personal Struggles
E-mail *struggles@maninthemirror.org* and one of our ministry team will get back to you.

Company Address
Man in the Mirror; 180 Wilshire Blvd.; Casselberry, FL 32707; USA
Phone: 407-472-2100; Toll Free 800-929-2536; Fax: 407-331-7839

LIFE'S SEASONS

There is a time for everything,
and a season for every activity
   under heaven:
a time to be born and a time to die,
a time to plant and a time to uproot,
a time to kill and a time to heal,
a time to tear down and a time to build,
a time to weep and a time to laugh,
a time to mourn and a time to dance,
a time to scatter stones and a time to
   gather them,
a time to embrace and a time to refrain,
a time to search and a time to give up,
a time to keep and a time to throw away,
a time to tear and a time to mend,
a time to be silent and a time to speak,
a time to love and a time to hate,
a time for war and a time for peace.
                    –Ecclesiastes 3:1-8

The Season of Crisis

WEEK 1

BURNOUT

Oswald Chambers wrote that most men have their own morality well within their grasp. That coincides with my experience. Since becoming a follower of Jesus Christ in the early 1970s, I have never really struggled with choices between good and evil. Of course, I've made thousands of errors in judgment, but I have had my morality well in hand.

The problem with leading a moral life is that we can deceive ourselves into thinking our good choices are also God's will. I learned the hard way that just because an idea is good and not evil does not necessarily mean it is "God." There is a huge difference between a *good* idea and a *God* idea.

Not knowing the difference between a good idea and a God idea got me into a heap of trouble. For the first 10 years of my spiritual journey, I lived my life by my own best thinking. I believe it was God's will for me to be a real estate developer—a calling. However, when I would evaluate a business deal, I would first decide whether or not the numbers penciled out, and only after I had already decided what I wanted to do, I would pray and ask God to work it out: "Lord, if You will just make this deal work out, I'll split the profits with You, and we'll both be better off!" It was "plan, then pray." I never really gave Him the opportunity to lead my life. Instead, I asked Him to follow me.

Henry Blackaby, in his workbook, *Experiencing God*, suggests that we "find out where God is working and join Him there." I'm afraid that in "our time" we are more likely to say, "Here I am working, God. Won't you come join me here?" Can you see how one approach puts God at the center while the other approach puts man at the center?

For this week, we are going to zero in on one kind of crisis that results from a man-centered approach to life: long-term burnout. Long-term burnout leaves men drained—emotionally, physically, psychologically, and spiritually. It is not momentary, fleeting, or sudden. It is often a midlife thing, although not limited to that time. Jim Conway's research for his book *Men in Mid-life Crisis* revealed that men have midlife crises from age 30 well into their 50s. Yet, I remember well a swollen-eyed man in his late 60s suffering from burnout. "I've lost my direction," he said.

WEEK 1, BURNOUT

Often the problem is that reality has set in. A man has had the thought, "It's just not going to happen the way I planned," even though he can't quite accept it yet. Or, as Jim Conway said, "I feel like a vending machine. Someone pushes a button and out comes _____." (Feel free to insert your own answers here. Smile.)

This week our objectives will be to:
- Discover the symptoms and problems leading to long-term burnout.
- Understand how sowing and reaping negative things can reap a harvest of crises.
- Explore the basic values and assumptions by which we live our lives.
- Face realistically our expectations, making certain we are not setting ourselves up for failure.
- Examine our purpose in life and see how it lines up with God's will for us.

I want to encourage you to spend time in prayer, carefully read the Scriptures suggested, and let God's Spirit guide and direct you.

★ **DAY 1** ★
The Symptoms in a Time of Crisis

★ **DAY 2** ★
Root Problems of Burnout

★ **DAY 3** ★
Values, What's Important?

★ **DAY 4** ★
Expectations, What's Due?

★ **DAY 5** ★
A Sense of Purpose, and Unresolved Issues

Memorize and meditate on this Scripture passage each day:

"Come to me, all you who are weary and burdened, and I will give you rest. Take my yoke upon you and learn from me, for I am gentle and humble in heart, and you will find rest for your souls" (Matthew 11:28-29).

DAY 1

THE SYMPTOMS IN A TIME OF CRISIS

Following a man-centered approach in my real estate dealings, I built a Tower of Babel and made a name for myself. Then, in 1986, I "hit the wall." The Tax Reform Act of 1986 threw me into a season of crisis. Things became so dismal that I didn't know how to pray. When I met with my weekly prayer partner, he asked how he should pray for me. I said, "Ken, all I can think of is to pray that God will grant me strength, courage, hope, grace, and mercy. If He grants me those five things, I can make it through."

Briefly describe a time in your life when you "hit the wall" in your work, relationships, marriage, or spiritual life.

_____

_____

Which of the following factors helped bring about that situation? (Check all that apply.)

- ❏ Marriage
- ❏ Death of a loved one
- ❏ Parents
- ❏ Friends having problems
- ❏ Other: _____
- ❏ Children
- ❏ Job
- ❏ School
- ❏ Wilderness experience with God
- ❏ Health problems
- ❏ Church conflict
- ❏ Money problems

How did you react? _____

Except for a period in 1987 when I thought everything would work out, I had to live each day from May 1986 to October 1993—more than seven years—with the possibility of going bankrupt. It was as if I was under a giant sword of Damocles suspended by a slender horse hair, and I knew that at any moment that slender thread could snap and it would be over for me. Ironically, the most productive years of my personal ministry were simultaneously taking place.

WEEK 1, CRISIS AND RENEWAL

It would have been easy to throw in the towel and give up. No one would have blamed me. The odds looked insurmountable. Yet, somewhere deep within me I sensed God calling me to fight for survival and not give up. I can't say I ever felt like I knew He would deliver me, but I can say I always sensed I knew I should never give up.

Thousands of times during those seven years, the pressure was too much. I simply couldn't visualize how to make it through one more day. Sometimes we couldn't pay our vendors on time. Sometimes we could not pay our mortgages on time. There were vendor work outs. Vender negotiations. More layoffs. The anxiety was devastating. It was embarrassing. It was humiliating. It was humbling.

Perhaps you, too, have faced the temptation to quit, or to "check out" of your situation. How do you respond to crisis? Put an x on each line to indicate how you respond.

Despairing							Hopeful
Withdrawn							Involved
Debilitated							Energized

In the long-term, God spared me from bankruptcy. But I came to realize two things. First, if I had gone bankrupt, I would have deserved it. It was only the kindness of God's grace working in me to stay the course that resulted in deliverance. Second, there were no guarantees that I would be spared. Many wonderful men are forced into bankruptcy. There is no disgrace in declaring bankruptcy *if you have done everything humanly possible to avoid it.*

It is interesting that I spent seven years piling up debt, and it took seven years to get out. Some crises come suddenly; others develop long-term. Some can be resolved quickly; others take a long time. And some problems, like the death of a child or visiting arrangements for children living with an ex-wife in another state, simply don't have solutions—we have to learn to live with them. This is a difficult reality to accept in an optimistic culture that often believes anything can be fixed given enough hard work.

THE SEASONS OF CRISIS AND RENEWAL

Crises are inevitable. The Chinese have an interesting word for crisis. They combine two characters—*danger* and *opportunity*—together in one word. Later on we'll explore the opportunities associated with this season. But right now, let's look at the chief danger—long-term burnout.

◆

**Long-term burnout leaves men drained
emotionally, physically, psychologically, and spiritually.**

Here are some symptoms of long-term burnout I have observed over the years. Perform a self-evaluation. Check the items in the following list that you experience regularly in your life.

- ❏ Physical ailments
- ❏ Lack of enthusiasm
- ❏ Easily fatigued during the day
- ❏ Tired at the beginning of a day
- ❏ Ineffective at tasks on the job
- ❏ Frustrated with my performance
- ❏ Depressed by my circumstances
- ❏ Confused about life's direction

- ❏ Highly anxious
- ❏ Short-tempered
- ❏ Friction at home
- ❏ Irritable
- ❏ Loss of focus
- ❏ Procrastinate
- ❏ Unhappy with my attitude
- ❏ Bored

Are more than just a few of these burnout symptoms in your life?

In the most severe form of burnout you may end up clinically depressed or even have suicidal thoughts. If things get this far, *it is serious*. If that is where you find yourself now or in the future, take steps to receive medical help and professional Christian counseling without delay.

You may not be burned out, and that is good. On the other hand, you may be on the way, and you may know you are—or maybe you don't. Perhaps you have been through a meltdown before. You may be in the middle of a burnout right now. One goal for this book is to help you avoid a burnout or, if you have already hit the wall, to walk away a better man. Because Somebody does care, Jesus cares. He said,

"Come to me, all you who are weary and burdened, and I will give you rest. Take my yoke upon you and learn from me, for I am gentle and humble in heart, and you will find rest for your souls. For my yoke is easy and my burden is light" (Matthew 11:28-30).

According to Strong's concordance, the word translated as *burdened* comes from a root that means "to load cargo onto a ship." The picture

WEEK 1, BURNOUT

is of someone who has loaded his boat with too much cargo, and now it's sinking.

One goal of this study is to help you avoid that feeling. But maybe you're already there. Maybe you thought your ship had come in, you launched into the deep, and now you're bailing water.

Read Matthew 11:28-30 again. Jesus invites you to come to Him. Then He gives specific instructions. Underline those instructions; circle the result that Jesus promises to those who are willing to do as He says.

Jesus promises *rest*. In fact, He mentions it twice in this one passage. Describe what *rest* means to you.

_____

Taking Jesus's yoke involves submission to His will and discipline. It means being His disciple. List two or three practical ways you can "take Jesus' yoke" and learn from Him.

_____

_____

Close today's study in prayer about those ways.

The Bottom Line
- Some crises come suddenly; others develop long-term. Some can be resolved quickly; others take a long time.
- Some problems don't have solutions—we have to learn to live with them.
- Long-term burnout leaves men drained—emotionally, physically, psychologically, and spiritually.
- Jesus cares about those suffering burnout; Jesus promises to give us rest.

DAY 2

ROOT PROBLEMS OF BURNOUT

How does a man get burned out? Whether he eats junk food or nutritious, healthy food, the difference is not immediately noticeable. In the same way, a season of crisis or burnout doesn't come suddenly.

◆

All burnout is the result of a long series of poor decisions.

The crisis builds one day at a time, one choice at a time. These choices don't seem big at the moment, but when compounded and added to thousands of similar decisions, they inevitably lead to crisis. We can choose our way, but not the results. Our choices have consequences.

Scripture talks about the principle of sowing and reaping in our lives.

"Do not be deceived: God cannot be mocked. A man reaps what he sows. The one who sows to please his sinful nature, from that nature will reap destruction; the one who sows to please the Spirit, from the Spirit will reap eternal life" (Galatians 6:7-8).

Because it takes time to reap a harvest, we are often deceived by sin. I can eat a chocolate sundae each day for the next month. Immediately upon gulping down that last bite of whipped cream and gooey syrup, I could run to the mirror and declare, "See, eating that sundae had no effect on me!" For a few weeks there would be no visible effect, but after enough time passed, I would begin to reap a harvest of increasing weight.

 Envision the harvest a man might receive from sowing each of the following seeds. In the column on the right, write a word or phrase that describes the harvest.

Sowing seeds of...	Results in a harvest of...
Love	_____
Financial overspending	_____
Kindness	_____
Anger	_____
Generosity	_____
Frugality	_____

I hope you did not make this exercise too difficult. The words you listed in the second column should relate to the words in the first. If we sow love, we will reap a harvest of love. If we sow overspending, our harvest will be debt. Kindness bears the fruit of kindness, and so forth.

Not all crises result from our choices, like certain health problems or calamities beyond our control. But some crises are within our control, and these are the crises for which we are responsible.

🐾 Identify and describe a problem you are facing or have faced recently. How might you have avoided it by sowing differently months or years ago?

_____

_____

_____

Our basic assumptions about life, our worldview, determine what we sow from day to day. As we make choices based on our worldview, we are laying a foundation for the future. The basic assumptions we make about the nature of God, man, world, devil, sin, eternal life, and salvation determine our future. And how we build on that foundation determines whether we will stand or fall in times of crisis.

🐾 What are the basic assumptions, the bedrock values and beliefs, that govern your life? Complete each sentence below by writing a summary statement that reflects your basic beliefs and worldview.

I believe that ...

God is _____

Jesus is _____

The Holy Spirit is _____

Family is _____

THE SEASONS OF CRISIS AND RENEWAL

Sin is _____

Eternal life is _____

The most important thing in life is _____

Love is _____

Salvation is _____

Jesus says this about laying foundations in life:

"Therefore, everyone who hears these words of mine and puts them into practice is like a wise man who built his house on the rock. The rain came down, the streams rose, and the winds blew and beat against that house; yet it did not fall, because it had its foundation on the rock. But everyone who hears these words of mine and does not put them into practice is like a foolish man who built his house on sand. The rain came down, the streams rose, and the winds blew and beat against that house, and it fell with a great crash" (Matthew 7:24-27).

Are you building your foundation on the sand or the rock? Building a balanced, rewarding life depends on making right choices about career, family, money, and God. Poor choices lead to burnout and crisis. A tree is known by its fruit. Free-floating anger, workaholism, preoccupation with material things, selfishness in relationships, and other rotten fruit are surface problems. We can, through self-examination, discover why we do what we do. We can look at the roots we have put down. The rest of this week we will examine four root problems that lay groundwork for poor choices: values, expectations, purpose, and unresolved issues.

What are some of the fruit you are harvesting in your life and relationships right now? Galatians 5:19-26 contrasts the rotten fruit of sinful living with the good fruit of the Spirit. On this list of various rotten and good fruit, place a check mark on each line to indicate how often you see each fruit manifested in your life.

WEEK 1, BURNOUT

The Fruit	The Frequency of Seeing This Fruit in My Life				
	Never	Seldom	Occasionally	Often	Always
Impurity					
Over-indulgence					
Idolatry					
Hatred					
Jealousy					
Selfish ambition					
Divisiveness					
Envy					
Love					
Joy					
Peace					
Kindness					
Goodness					
Faithfulness					
Gentleness					
Self-control					

Close today by thanking God for the good fruit in your life.

The Bottom Line
- All burnout is the result of a long series of poor decisions.
- A crisis builds one day at a time, once choice at a time.
- The basic assumptions we make about the nature of God, man, world, devil, sin, eternal life and salvation determine our future.
- Building a balanced, rewarding life depends on making right choices about career, family, money, and God.

DAY 3

VALUES, WHAT'S IMPORTANT?

Our *values* answer the questions, "What's important?" and "What has worth?" What are the principles, standards, and beliefs we hold to be worthwhile? Values are what we consider important to us.

◆

Poor choices about our values can lead to a crisis.

In his early 30s, Mike had a life-changing experience with Jesus Christ. Mike grew deeply and intensely over the next two years. An important promotion came for Mike, and he began to devote himself to building a business. Over the next 10 years, Mike traveled extensively and missed most of the growing-up experiences of his two daughters. He developed an immoral lifestyle. To compensate for her loneliness, his wife turned to alcohol. Mike also began drinking. Finally, a divorce split his family, and Mike continued his immorality. Mike could no longer pray. He hit the wall in his job, his loss of family, and his spiritual life. In agony, Mike cried out, "God, where are You?" How does this happen? We lose direction for our lives when we choose the wrong values. We have a problem when we buy into the values of our *culture* instead of the *kingdom*.

Are your values based on our culture or on God's Kingdom? The following list includes five significant areas influenced by our values. Complete each statement to reveal what is most important to you. Look up and read each Scripture. Indicate on the continuum whether your values are very close or not close at all to these biblical values.

What's most important to me about ...

... my marriage (if you are married) is _____.
My values compared to biblical values of submission, love, and respect (Ephesians 5:21-23) are:

Very Close   Not Close at All

... **my family is** _____.
My values compared to biblical values of honor, obedience, and respect (Ephesians 6:1-4) are:

Very Close   Not Close at All

... **my faith is** _____.
My values compared to biblical values of righteousness, salvation, and belief in Christ (Romans 10:1-17) are:

Very Close   Not Close at All

... **my relationships with friends are** _____.
My values compared to biblical values of love, faithfulness, and trust (Proverbs 17:17, 18:24, 27:6) are:

Very Close   Not Close at All

... **my integrity is** _____.
My values compared to biblical values of uprightness (Psalm 25:21) are:

Very Close   Not Close at All

Go back over your list and circle those values most closely shaped by God's Word. Put a question mark by those values most closely shaped by culture. What does this reveal to you?

Our culture is the sum of society's behavioral patterns. It includes all the products of our work and thought. Culture affects how we think, what we believe, and the language we use. We cannot, nor should we, escape our culture. But it is of paramount importance that we understand it.

List 4 things important to people in your age group in our culture.

1. _____   3. _____

2. _____   4. _____

THE SEASONS OF CRISIS AND RENEWAL

There isn't necessarily a right or wrong answer to the preceding exercise. My list includes: careerism, individualism, consumerism, materialism, relativism, and pluralism. You could say that we have a bad case of the "isms," many of which challenge us to win at all costs, to glory in self-reliance, to choose possessions over people, and to tolerate beliefs and behaviors with which we disagree. Those kinds of culturally-formed values lead to pain. But God can use that for our good. The "pain" that brings us back to God is *grace*.

So, what is important to you? List your top four priorities.

1. _____   3. _____

2. _____   4. _____

Are you living by the values of God's Kingdom or our culture? List one significant value adjustment you need to make.

_____

What does God want you to do as a result of today's lesson?

_____

> **The Bottom Line**
> - We lose direction for our lives when we choose the wrong values.
> - We have a problem when we buy into values of our culture instead of God's Kingdom.
> - Culturally formed values lead to pain.
> - The "pain" that brings us back to God is *grace*.

DAY 4

EXPECTATIONS, WHAT'S DUE?

Our expectations show how we answer the questions, "What's due?" or "What can I expect?" Expectations are things we consider likely or certain to happen. We feel they are owed to us or due us. In short, we expect them.

What do you expect out of life? Rate the priority of each of the following areas from high (1) to low (7).
___ To be treated with dignity and respect by others.
___ To be loved and affirmed by others.
___ To make a respectable wage.
___ To own a home.
___ To drive a late model car of my choice.
___ To be spiritually mature.
___ Other: _____

Unrealistic or unmet expectations can lead to crisis. The problem we face is that our culture fosters high expectations, even rights. We end up thinking that to be happy, we need to hold down a particular kind of job; therefore, we need to earn a particular level of income; therefore, we need to live in a particular kind of house in a particular kind of neighborhood; and therefore we need to drive a particular kind of car; and all by a particular age. Why? Simply because that's what we are programmed to expect when we adopt expectations from our culture. For two years I have been pondering a sentence that I believe answers a lot of questions about life. I reproduce it here, but ask you not to read past it quickly. You may find it valuable to do as I have done and write it somewhere for long-term reflection. Here it is:

◆

All disappointment is the result of unmet expectations.

We most often approach the issue of expectations and rights from a worldview based in secular culture. But God's ways are not our ways and His thoughts are not our thoughts (see Isaiah 55:8).

This certainly shouldn't be a surprise, for Scripture recorded this fact long ago. Proverbs 13:12 notes, "Hope deferred makes the heart sick, but a longing fulfilled is a tree of life." The word translated *hope* literally means expectation.

Describe how a "deferred" or "unmet" expectation has led to disappointment in your life.

_____

_____

_____

So when we experience the disappointment of "hope deferred," it is crucial that we reevaluate our expectations in light of God's Word. We may need to lower some of them, or even cross some of them off the list all together. Romans 5:1-5 is a great place to begin our search for biblical expectations. It notes that if we've been justified by our faith in Christ and His sacrifice on our behalf, then we can expect to have peace with God. We can expect to gain access to grace. And we can expect that He will enable us to live in a way that glorifies Him.

That kind of expectation allows us to rejoice in difficult circumstances, because it allows us to trust more and more in Christ. The end result, then, is that "suffering produces perseverance; perseverance, character; and character, hope." And that kind of hope *never* disappoints, because it is based on the character of God and the eternal promise of His love, mercy, and grace.

The Old Testament puts it this way: "Though the fig tree does not bud and there are no grapes on the vines, though the olive crop fails and the fields produce no food, though there are no sheep in the pen and no cattle in the stalls, yet I will rejoice in the Lord, I will be joyful in God my Saviour" (Habakkuk 3:17-18).

WEEK 1, BURNOUT

🐾 The author of this passage was writing as a farmer in an agriculturally-based economy. Paraphrase this passage for your situation. For instance, you may want to write, "Even if my car is totalled in an accident that is not my fault ... ," or "Even if my house burns in an accident that is not my fault ... ," or "Even if I am passed over for a promotion at work ..."

_____

_____

Now that you have paraphrased that passage to fit your situation, mark an x on the continuum at the place that represents the ease with which you could legitimately say, "Yet will I rejoice in the Lord."

Very Easy   Extremely Difficult

Does this mean we shouldn't make any plans or hold any expectations for the future? No. It just means our plans must be secondary to God's will, and our expectations must be aligned with His word.

The Bible says, "Every good gift and every perfect gift is from above, and comes down from the Father of lights" (James 1:17, NKJV). Too often we don't show gratitude for the many blessings we receive, and we become selfishly angered over the blessings we don't receive. Instead, we should receive everything with gratitude and humbly trust God when we don't get what we want.

🐾 What does God want you to do as a result of today's study?

_____

_____

_____

Write a prayer surrendering your expectations and rights to God.

_____

_____

_____

_____

The Bottom Line
- All disappointment is the result of unmet expectations.
- Expectations that are rooted in God's character and eternal love never disappoint.
- Our plans must be secondary to God's will, and our expectations must be aligned with His Word.

DAY 5

A SENSE OF PURPOSE, AND UNRESOLVED ISSUES

> Our purpose answers the questions:
> "What's the point?"
> "Why do I exist?"
> "What am I here for?"

Charles Barkley said in a 1994 television interview that the purpose of his life—his reason to exist—was to win an National Basketball Association title. There are three problems with this kind of thinking.

1. He is seeking glory, not meaning.
2. That purpose is not big enough for a lifetime.
3. He cannot control the outcome.

Get ready, Charles. The demons of disillusionment are coming your way.

Let's approach it from this perspective. To whom would you turn to discover the purpose for (write your answer):

- a car? _____
- a watch? _____
- a computer? _____

I hope you wrote down the obvious answers. The best person to tell us the purpose of something is the person who created that thing. An automaker, watchmaker, or computer programmer could tell us the purpose behind those things. Likewise, the One who knows the purpose of a man is the One who created man. Listen to what God says, "Let us make man in our image, in our likeness" (Genesis 1:26). So, purpose is grounded in whom we were created to be—not in what we think, plan, or devise.

In one sentence, write what you know to be God's purpose for your life:

_____

_____

Compare what you have written to what Scripture says about man's purpose and design. Read each passage and briefly list man's purpose.

SCRIPTURE	MAN'S PURPOSE
The Great Commission "Therefore go and make disciples of all nations, baptizing them in the name of the Father and of the Son and of the Holy Spirit, and teaching them to obey everything I have commanded you. And surely I am with you always, to the very end of the age" (Matthew 28:19-20).	_____
Cultural Mandate God blessed them and said to them, "Be fruitful and increase in number; fill the earth and subdue it. Rule over the fish of the sea and the birds of the air and over every living creature that moves on the ground" (Genesis 1:28).	_____
Great Commandment "Love the Lord your God with all your heart and with all your soul and with all your mind" (Matthew 22:37).	_____
New Commandment "A new command I give you: Love one another. As I have loved you, so you must love one another" (John 13:34).	_____

The Westminster Confession centuries ago declared that the chief end of man was to glorify God. What a purpose! Once we determine that God gets the glory in our lives, we can move ahead with living our purpose in life. All glory is reserved for God. Certainly we all need encouragement from others. But we live not to receive the praises of men, but to glorify God. Who gets the glory in your life?

WEEK 1, BURNOUT

◆

The purpose of our lives ought to be based on the *quality* of our *character* and *conduct*, not on the *quantity* of our *circumstances* over which we have no or limited control.

The Quality of Character and Conduct

The only things we control completely, by God's grace, are our character and conduct. We control the character qualities of integrity, our love for God and people, and humility. We control how we conduct ourselves in speech, kindness, and diligence. Surely these will contribute to the quality of our circumstances, but not with a one-to-one correlation. A wrong orientation at this point surely leads to crisis.

Philippians 4:8-9 lists for us the qualities of a Christian's thought life.

"Finally, brothers, whatever is true, whatever is noble, whatever is right, whatever is pure, whatever is lovely, whatever is admirable—if anything is excellent or praiseworthy—think about such things. Whatever you have learned or received or heard from me, or seen in me—put it into practice. And the God of peace will be with you."

Galatians 5:22 reveals the fruit that the Spirit of God produces in our lives through our conduct, "The fruit of the Spirit is love, joy, peace, patience, kindness, goodness, faithfulness, gentleness and self-control. Against such things there is no law."

Unresolved Issues

Most of us get so busy that we have unresolved issues. If we pretend certain problems will go away, we may be setting ourselves up for a crisis. For some, our fathers have never given us their approval. Or other key relationships may go unresolved in the pedal-to-the-floor race to keep on top of our responsibilities.

Some unresolved issues relate to *tasks*, but by far the majority deal with *relationships*. We tend to take care of our tasks at the expense of our relationships. In the process, we wound people and damage those we love the most. We don't express remorse or seek forgiveness.

 What, or better yet, *who* are the unresolved issues in your life?

THE SEASONS OF CRISIS AND RENEWAL

If that person is no longer available to you because of death or another type of separation, you may have to simply accept the pain, learn from it, and resolve to apply those lessons to your other relationships. But, if that person is still accessible, what can you do to resolve this situation?

_____

_____

Over time, making wrong moral choices in our values, expectations, purpose, and unresolved issues can lead to crises. Where have you been making poor choices? Ask God to help you address the root problems in your life. Pray for God's wisdom in making right decisions about values, expectations, purpose, and unresolved issues in your life.

> **The Bottom Line**
> - The purpose of our lives ought to be based on the *quality* of our *character* and *conduct*, not on the *quantity* of our *circumstances* over which we have no or limited control.
> - The only things we control completely, by God's grace, are our character and conduct.
> - If we pretend that unresolved issues will just go away, we may be setting ourselves up for a crisis.
> - Some unresolved issues relate to *tasks*, but by far the majority relate to *relationships*.

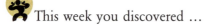This week you discovered …
- the symptoms and problems leading to long-term burnout.
- how to make moral choices in your values, expectations, purpose, and unresolved issues that will steer you away from crises.

What does God want you to do as a result of this week's study?

_____

WEEK 2

THE DARK NIGHT OF THE SOUL

The journey back from the world of Cultural Christianity to the kingdom of Biblical Christianity will often pass through what St. John of the Cross called "the dark night of the soul."

God will often lead a "soul" who has gone astray onto the path of "dark contemplation and aridity, wherein it seems to be lost." It is a time full of darkness and trials, constraints and temptations. Your season of crisis may well be a dark night for your soul.

This week you will learn to lean more fully on Jesus Christ through this difficult time of life, knowing that the end result will be God's glory and your good.

Our objective will be to:
- Understand the "dark night of the soul."
- Reveal how the root problems of Cultural Christianity and the self-help gospel lead us into the spiritual, physical, and emotional desert.
- Discover how we can accept responsibility for the problem and solution to our self-made crises, and the way out of them.

Commit yourself to spending daily time this week in God's Word and in prayer. Read all the Scripture passages suggested. Seek God's leading and truth in your study.

THE SEASONS OF CRISIS AND RENEWAL

★ DAY 1 ★ The Root Problem of Cultural Christianity

★ DAY 2 ★ Understanding Cultural Christianity

★ DAY 3 ★ Accepting Responsibility for the Problem

★ DAY 4 ★ Accepting Responsibility for the Solution

★ DAY 5 ★ The Way Back

As you walk through your daily studies, I invite you to memorize and meditate on these Scripture verses each day.

Therefore, I urge you, brothers, in view of God's mercy, to offer your bodies as living sacrifices, holy and pleasing to God—this is your spiritual act of worship. Do not conform any longer to the pattern of the world, but be transformed by the renewing of your mind (Romans 12:1-2).

I pray that as you understand the crises in your life, you will learn to lean even more on the Lord.

DAY 1

THE ROOT PROBLEM OF CULTURAL CHRISTIANITY

One morning as I was sitting in the rubble of my collapsed empire, trying to discover where I had gone astray, a thought came to mind that I believe is the most important lesson I have ever learned. There is a God we want, and there is a God who is. They are not the same God.

◆

The turning point of our lives is when we stop seeking the God we want and start seeking the God who is.

God is who He is. No amount of wanting Him to be someone or something else will change anything. Our task is not to change God but to be changed by God. Our task is not to reinvent God in the imagination but to discover the God who is already there. God will do what God will do. To think we can outsmart God is pure tomfoolery.

Cultural Christianity simply means to seek the God (or gods) we want and not the God who is. It is clinging to our idols instead of smashing them to smithereens. Here is a great problem: Men become **Cultural Christians** when they are not **Biblical Christians**.

The Bible has much to say about the **God who is.** Scripture reveals how God does not conform to our ideas about Him. Read each passage and briefly describe the **God who is.**

Passage	The God Who Is...
"As the heavens are higher than the earth, so are my ways higher than your ways and my thoughts than your thoughts (Isaiah 55:9).	
"I am the Lord your God, who brought you out of Egypt, out of the land of slavery. You shall have no other gods before me" (Exodus 20:2-3).	

THE SEASONS OF CRISIS AND RENEWAL

Acknowledge and take to heart this _____
day that the Lord is God in heaven _____
above and on the earth below. _____
There is no other _____
(Deuteronomy 4:39). _____

Those verses demonstrate God's right to rule our lives. A Biblical Christian accepts that and submits. But when a man is a Cultural Christian, he has divided his loyalties between God and the things of this world. Matthew 6:24 says you can't serve both God and money. But that's just one example. The bottom line is that you can't serve both God and any other person or thing.

Below is a circle representing the different areas of your life. Shade in those segments that you have surrendered fully to the Lord.

WEEK 2, THE DARK NIGHT OF THE SOUL

If there is an area not shaded, what must you do to bring that under the lordship of Jesus?

In *The Ascent of Mount Carmel*, St. John of the Cross wrote, "When the will of a man is affectioned to one thing, he prizes it more than any other; although some other things may be better."[1] If our affections are on worldly things rather than on Jesus, we have not chosen the better. What must God do to break the stranglehold that the affections of the world have on a man?

In the wilderness God fed the wandering Israelites with manna. But they wanted more—they wanted meat. St. John of the Cross wrote, "They failed to find in the manna all the sweetness and strength that they could wish, not because it was not contained in the manna, but because they desired some other thing."[2] What must God do to make a man not want some other thing?

For a man to become a Biblical Christian, his desire for the things of this world must die. He must crucify, or mortify, the desires of his flesh.

In the introduction to this week's study, I cited Romans 12:1-2. Refer back to that page and re-read those verses. According to that passage, we are not to be _____ to the things of this world. Instead, we are to be _____ by the _____.

Few men can do this on their own. Hence, the dark night of the soul.

Before my own dark night of the soul, I remember hating my sin. But I also remember being powerless to overcome it. The dark night of the soul was God's gracious gesture to turn me back to Him. He helped me crucify my ambition, purify my thought life, and correct my motives. I wouldn't dare say I have attained anything near this, but at least now I desire it with all my heart.

Do not chafe against the dark night of your soul. You may be on that path because you have been a Cultural Christian or for some other reason. Whatever the reason, the dark night of your soul is God's kindness to empty your soul of self. Look to *attend* your worldly affairs without becoming *entangled* in them. Seek to abandon yourself to God. This dark night will lead you as surely as the brightest light.

THE SEASONS OF CRISIS AND RENEWAL

🐾 Briefly describe a wilderness experience you have had and what you learned about God's grace in that "dark night of the soul."

_____

_____

Below are some attitudes and actions you can take on your part to surrender fully to the Lord as you pass through your "dark night of the soul." These are part of making your body a living sacrifice to God. Close today's study by circling one you need to implement in your life.
- Empty your soul of self (Galatians 2:20).
- Become detached from the world (Matthew 6:24).
- Abandon yourself to the Lord (Mark 8:34-36).
- Set God's Kingdom as your life's priority (Matthew 6:33).
- Seek God's presence, not just His gifts (Psalm 27:8).
- Turn away from sin (2 Chronicles 7:14).
- Praise God in the midst of adversity (Psalm 71:10-17).
- Find someone who will hold you accountable for your actions and attitudes (James 5:16).

The Bottom Line
- **The turning point of our lives is when we stop seeking the God we want and start seeking the God who is.**
- **Men become Cultural Christians when they are not Biblical Christians.**
- **You can't serve both God and any other person or thing.**
- **The dark night of your soul is God's kindness to empty your soul of self.**

---

[1] St. John of the Cross, *The Ascent of Mount Carmel* (New York: Triumph Books), 30.
[2] Ibid.

DAY 2

UNDERSTANDING CULTURAL CHRISTIANITY

Like saltwater intrusion into a freshwater bay, Cultural Christianity pollutes Biblical Christianity slowly, over time, with little observable notice. It is difficult to defeat an enemy you can't see and don't understand.

◆

Understanding Cultural Christianity is the first step to leaving it behind.

The problem with Cultural Christianity is twofold.

1. Many men never understand what the Bible says. Men often have a respect for the Bible but no knowledge of its contents. The Bible presents a detailed picture of who we are, who God is, and how we should live in response. Biblical history shows when men did not study, understand, and obey God's Word, they simply did what seemed right in their own eyes (see Judges 17:6; 21:25). The Bible says a man is a slave of whatever has mastered him (see 1 Peter 2:19). The best line of defense is to be mastered by the Bible.

Check the things in the following list that you are already doing. Circle one thing you need to start or increase in your life.
- ❏ Listening attentively and regularly to biblical sermons.
- ❏ Learning the Word through a Bible study class or group.
- ❏ Teaching God's Word to others.
- ❏ Taking time daily to read and study God's Word.
- ❏ Memorizing and meditating on God's Word.
- ❏ Praying and allowing the Holy Spirit to teach the Word in my heart.
- ❏ Allowing a small group of men to hold me accountable for studying my Bible and living out what I learn.

2. Many men rebel against what they do know from the Bible and live by their own best thinking. Truth is never determined by a majority vote. Proverbs 14:12 declares, "There is a way that seems right to a man, but in the end it leads to death."

THE SEASONS OF CRISIS AND RENEWAL

Read in your Bible the story of Saul in 1 Samuel 15. List the steps to rebellion as described in the verses indicated.

1. Saul _____ the King and the livestock (v. 9).
2. Saul _____ from God. (v. 11)
3. Saul did not _____ God's instructions. (v. 11)
4. Saul set up a monument in his _____. (v. 12)
5. In describing what he had done, Saul _____. (v. 15)
6. Denying his disobedience, Saul claimed to have _____ God. (v. 20)

(Answers: 1. spared; 2. turned away; 3. carry out; 4. own honor; 5. lied; 6. obeyed)

In studying Saul's rebellion against God, we can clearly see steps to rebellion.

1. Turning away from God.
2. Doing what's right in man's eyes.
3. Disobeying God's Word.
4. Seeking personal honor and glory.
5. Being proud and self-centered.
6. Denying wrongdoing.
7. Being unwilling to repent.
8. Rebelling against God and His servants.

King Saul's basic sin was his determination to follow his own way rather than God's. Many men fall into that trap. We know the Word, but we ignore it and advance our own opinions instead.

Does our opinion about the meaning of life, the nature of man, the character of God, and the way of salvation really matter if God has another opinion?   ❑ yes   ❑ no

Explain your answer.

_____

_____

The Self-Help Gospel

In American culture today, the self-help gospel is a dominant message. The self-help gospel will always lead men to become Cultural Christians. Cultural Christians are self-made men.

The self-help gospel blends the human potential movement and selected Christian values. It suggests that self-esteem and success, not salvation, are the purpose of faith. Cultural Christians confess belief in God and Jesus, but they tend to not accept the authority of the Bible and to make up their own religion as they go.

In days gone by, a person had to confess faith in Christ before joining the church. Not so today. Because of low to no prerequisites for joining the body of Christ, many churches are top-heavy with people who don't know God personally. On top of that, because of a low view of God in many churches, there is a plethora of Cultural Christians—some of whom we might call mature infants in Christ, and some don't even know Him at all. They know *about* God, but they don't know *Him*.

A *U.S. News and World Report* cover story reported that...
- 95 percent of Americans believe in God.
- 71 percent of college graduates believe the Bible is the inspired Word of God.
- 62 percent of college graduates say they attend religious services.
- 46 percent of college graduates say they are born again.[1]

These statistics seem to indicate that we have a religious revival in America. However, it is not a *spiritual* revival, but a *demographic* revival. It has a form of godliness but does not depend on faith in the finished work of the historical Jesus Christ for redemption. In fact, redemption from sin and death is rarely mentioned in Cultural Christianity.

Cultural Christians don't set out to make God into the God they want. More often than not, they are simply swept along by the most popular teachings of the day.

Evaluate the influence of this self-help gospel on you. Put an x on each line that represents how often you hear each statement.

God helps those who help themselves.

Often			Sometimes			Never

Think positively and things will happen positively.

Often   Sometimes   Never

If you have enough faith, your dreams will come true.

Often   Sometimes   Never

Try harder and you can achieve any goal you set.

Often   Sometimes   Never

Perhaps you have been too influenced by Cultural Christianity; you need a new paradigm. In closing, pray this prayer:

Almighty God, I confess that in many ways I have been a Cultural Christian. At times I have not understood your Word, and sometimes, when I did understand, I chose to disobey. I don't want to live by my own thinking anymore. I want to follow you. In Jesus' Name, Amen.

The Bottom Line

- Understanding Cultural Christianity is the first step to leaving it behind.
- Men often have a respect for but no knowledge of the Bible.
- Many men rebel against the Bible and live by their own best thinking.
- The self-help gospel always leads men to become Cultural Christians.
- Cultural Christianity has a form of godliness but does not depend on faith in the finished work of Jesus Christ.

---

[1]"Spiritual America, In God We Trust," *U.S. News and World Report*, 4 April 1994, 50, 53-54.

DAY 3

ACCEPTING RESPONSIBILITY FOR THE PROBLEM

There are two distinct approaches to our faith. They lead to inevitably different results. Ron Nash said it well: "I don't mind if people want to make up a new religion. I just wish they wouldn't call it Christianity."

Paradigm One: The Self-help Gospel. The self-help gospel is pure Cultural Christianity. Its ultimate purpose is personal fulfillment; to pursue the God we want.

Paradigm Two: The Gospel of the Kingdom. The Gospel of the Kingdom is Biblical Christianity. Its ultimate purpose is to usher in the Kingdom of God; to pursue the God who is.

◆

**The object of the self-help gospel is to pursue the God we want.
The object of the gospel of the Kingdom is
to pursue the God who is.**

Cultural Christianity
1. The God I want.
2. Try to be good.
3. Build a better world.
4. Faith is another item on my checklist of things "to do."
5. Truth is relative and conditional, determined by popular opinion or self-interests.
6. Ultimate purpose in life is personal fulfillment

Biblical Christianity
1. The God who is.
2. Admit sin and weakness.
3. Make disciples.
4. Faith is surrender to Jesus Christ as Savior and Lord.
5. Truth is absolute and rooted in the nature and character of God.
6. Ultimate purpose in life is to glorify God.

 Go through both lists. Compare each point with its counterpart. For each number, circle the point that best reflects your personal beliefs. In which column did you circle the most items?

❑ Cultural Christianity   ❑ Biblical Christianity

THE SEASONS OF CRISIS AND RENEWAL

As we learned earlier this week, God will sometimes allow a Cultural Christian to pass through a "dark night of the soul" to help him adopt a new paradigm. Two steps in particular will help you pass through the dark night of the soul and come out on the other side. 1) Accept full responsibility for the problem. 2) Accept full responsibility for the solution. We'll look at that second step tomorrow. For now, let's consider the first.

Taking responsibility does not begin with sincerity. The curse of the Cultural Christian is his sincerity. I'm convinced American churches hold millions of men hostage to their own sincerity. They are good men, but they are trusting in their own good deeds. Our relationship with God depends not on our good deeds but on our faith and trust in Christ.

Read Ephesians 2:8-9 below. Briefly summarize this teaching in your own words.

"For it is by grace you have been saved, through faith—and this not from yourselves, it is the gift of God—not by works, so that no one can boast."

_____

_____

Cultural Christianity is, in a word, sin. To seek the God or gods we want is idolatry, and idolatry is sin. How does Biblical Christianity teach us to deal with sin? Read the following Scripture passages and briefly summarize in the right column what we are to do with sin.

If we confess our sins, he is faithful and just and will forgive us our sins and purify us from all unrighteousness (1 John 1:9).	_____ _____ _____
Peter replied, "Repent and be baptized, every one of you, in the name of Jesus Christ for the forgiveness of your sins" (Acts 2:38).	_____ _____ _____

WEEK 2, THE DARK NIGHT OF THE SOUL

Being sorry for sin is not enough. When we sin, the Bible calls us to repent. To repent means to turn around, to go in the opposite direction. When we have sinned against God, we must express genuine remorse and then repent or pledge to act differently. There is a difference between worldly sorrow (merely feeling sorry for yourself) and godly sorrow: "Godly sorrow brings repentance that leads to salvation and leaves no regret, but worldly sorrow brings death" (2 Corinthians 7:10).

We need to repent of Cultural Christianity. We need to acknowledge our sin and take responsibility for the way we have lived.

Review today's lesson. What one statement or Scripture passage spoke most to you? Write it below.

_____

_____

What does God want you to do as a result of today's study?

_____

_____

> **The Bottom Line**
> - The object of the self-help gospel is to pursue the God we want. The object of the gospel of the Kingdom is to pursue the God who is.
> - The paradigms of Cultural Christianity and Biblical Christianity are opposite in almost every way.

DAY 4

ACCEPTING RESPONSIBILITY FOR THE SOLUTION

Under the leadership of Bill Hybels, Willow Creek Community Church near Chicago has grown from 125 people in 1975 to more than 14,000 today—one of America's largest. Bill was a sought-after speaker, writer, consultant, and chaplain for the Chicago Bears for 5 years. He kept his eye on two gauges in his life. First, he closely watched his *spiritual* gauge by asking, "How am I doing spiritually?" He always kept this area of his life in tune. The second gauge he watched closely was the *physical* gauge, "How am I doing physically?" He kept his body healthy.

One day while preparing for some messages, Bill's mind went dry, and he found himself sobbing. He checked his gauges. No problem. Yet, he broke down several more times in the coming weeks. After self-examination, Bill discovered he had a third gauge—the *emotional* gauge. It was on empty. Since then, Bill has identified warning signs that let him know his emotional resources are near empty. He has accepted responsibility to find and implement God's solution for his dark night of the soul.

◆

After assuming responsibility for the problem, we must assume full responsibility for the solution.

An important part of the solution is spiritual, physical, and emotional rest. We need to take the responsibility to monitor gauges for these crucial areas of our lives. When we see the gauges moving toward "empty," we *must* also take the responsibility to stop and refuel. Let's examine each one of these gauges in our lives, beginning with the spiritual.

Indicate on the graphs below the level of your...

spiritual tank:
Empty — Full

physical tank:
Empty — Full

emotional tank:
Empty — Full

WEEK 2, THE DARK NIGHT OF THE SOUL

✝ Below is a checklist of things that fill our spiritual tanks. Check those that are a regular part of your life.
- ❑ Worship
- ❑ Studying God's Word
- ❑ Meditating on God's Word
- ❑ Witnessing to others
- ❑ Prayer
- ❑ Fellowshipping with other believers
- ❑ Serving others
- ❑ Memorizing God's Word
- ❑ Praising and thanking the Lord
- ❑ Being silent before God

If only a few are checked, what will you do to take responsibility for being filled spiritually? Go back to the list and circle what the Holy Spirit prompts you to do.

✝ What about your physical gauge? Some men brag about never having a day off or taking a vacation. They are simply foolish. Below is a checklist. Check those that are a regular part of your life.
- ❑ Exercise
- ❑ Adequate sleep
- ❑ Enjoyable use of leisure time
- ❑ Vacation time to enjoy wife, family, and friends
- ❑ Proper and healthy diet
- ❑ Time off each week
- ❑ Refuse to bring work home
- ❑ A 15-minute minivacation every day

If only a few of the above are checked, what will you do to take responsibility for improving your physical life? Go back to the list and circle one thing you will do to improve physically.

✝ Finally, what about your emotional gauge? Below and continuing on the next page is a list of ways to fill your emotional tank. Check those that happen regularly in your life.
- ❑ Affirmation from my wife
- ❑ Affirmation from my children
- ❑ Affirmation at work
- ❑ Intimacy with my wife
- ❑ Enjoyable and meaningful activities with my children
- ❑ Prayer with my wife
- ❑ Accountability to another Christian man or group of men
- ❑ An interesting hobby or other diversion
- ❑ Rest from draining tasks and relationships

THE SEASONS OF CRISIS AND RENEWAL

❏ Meaningful service through my church
❏ Read a novel
❏ Proper use of spiritual gifts
❏ Living as a "called" man vs. a "driven" man

If you only checked a few of these, which areas need to grow more in your life? Go back to the list and circle the areas you will pursue to have your emotional tank filled.

My parents instilled a strong work ethic in me. I love to work. Work is my hobby. I would rather work than eat, and I often do. As a result, I tend to run myself down emotionally. One habit I have gotten into helps. When I feel like throwing my hands up in the air, I will often quit and take the rest of the day off.

The forgotten priority of our culture is rest. We excel at our tasks, but we find it extremely difficult to slow down. We may even feel a twinge of guilt when we relax. But rest is a priority with God.

Read the following passages and summarize how each one applies to your life.

Remember the Sabbath day by keeping it holy. Six days you shall labor and do all your work, but the seventh day is a Sabbath to the Lord your God. On it you shall not do any work (Exodus 20:8-10).

_____

He makes me lie down in green pastures,
he leads me beside quiet waters,
he restores my soul (Psalm 23:2-3).

_____

The apostles gathered around Jesus and reported to him all they had done and taught. Then, because so many people were coming and

_____

WEEK 2, THE DARK NIGHT OF THE SOUL

going that they did not even have
a chance to eat, he said to them,
"Come with me by yourselves to a
quiet place and get some rest"
(Mark 6:30-31).

_____
_____
_____
_____
_____

God has commanded us to take time to rest. Are you obeying Him? You must take responsibility to find God's solution to your problem and then to implement it. I encourage you to set aside a block of time for physical rest, one for emotional rejuvenation, and one for spiritual renewal. Pencil them in on your calendar sometime in the next month.

Ask the Holy Spirit to bless those times you have set aside and to renew every aspect of your life. Close today's study by writing a prayer expressing that and acknowledging God's work in you.

_____
_____
_____

The Bottom Line
- After assuming responsibility for the problem, we also must assume full responsibility for the solution.
- We must accept responsibility for monitoring gauges for the three primary areas of life: spiritual, physical, and emotional.
- When we see the gauges moving toward "empty," we must take responsibility to stop and refuel.
- The forgotten priority of our culture is rest.

DAY 5

THE WAY BACK

One day I was bringing my father-in-law up-to-date on my "dark night of the soul." The pressure had drained me of all enthusiasm. Food did not appeal to me. I walked and talked like a mummy. I was depressed. I figured I would never again be happy. I was drained of joy. I was a wreck—an emotional, physical, and psychological burnout.

After I explained my situation and how I felt, he said, "Pat, two years from now your joy will return, and the enthusiasm you have always felt for your work will come back."

I remember two distinct thoughts coming to me. First, *No way. I will never, ever again enjoy what I'm doing. It will never happen.* The second thought I had was, *Why does it have to take so long?*

◆

**There is no easy way out of a long-term crisis;
it takes time to recharge and heal.**

God has anticipated your season of crisis and the dark night of your soul. God knows you need to be healed and restored in your relationship with Him and others. Don't be too hard on yourself. Forgiveness is immediate. Restoration often takes days, weeks, months, even years.

God's Word is a balm for your burnout and pain. Into your darkness will come the light of His Word. The book of Psalms could easily be called *The Burnout Book.* Discover this for yourself. I have listed below Psalms that address some of the significant feelings we have when on the way out of the wilderness. You may not have time to read them all, but I encourage you to read three or four of them now and come back to the list as you face your wilderness experience.

Hope (Psalm 33)
Joy (Psalm 126:3-6)
Healing (Psalm 103)
Security (Psalm 112)

Strength (Psalm 28)
Forgiveness (Psalm 51:1-9)
Blessing (Psalm 1)
Depression (Psalm 40:1-3)

WEEK 2, THE DARK NIGHT OF THE SOUL

Comfort (Psalm 23:1-6)
Peace (Psalm 37)
Protection (Psalm 91)

Identity (Psalm 139)
God's Word (Psalm 119:9-16)
Restoration (Psalm 80)

As you use the Psalms (and other passages) to bring healing and provide strength and encouragement, consider these suggestions:
- Read the passage out loud.
- Pray through the passage.
- Sing the passage.
- Memorize a key verse.
- Share the text with a Christian friend or someone in need.
- Underline key words or verses that speak to you.
- Circle the verse that ministers directly to your need.
- Put an exclamation mark (!) by the verse needing action right away.

Beginning next week we will explore the Season of Renewal. This season will further describe how God brings you through healing after a crisis. You may not see the end to your crisis right now. Nonetheless, God promises that He will see you through.

> **The Bottom Line**
> - There is no easy way out of a long-term crisis; it takes time to recharge and heal.
> - Forgiveness is immediate; restoration often takes days, weeks, months, even years.

 This week you discovered ...
- how to face the "dark night of the soul."
- how to accept responsibility for the problem and solution to your self-made crises, and the way out of them.

What does God want you to do in response to this week's study?

_____

Recite Romans 12:1-2 as a closing thought for the week.

THE SEASON OF REFLECTION

REFLECTING ON THIS SEASON

1. The most important truth I learned for my spiritual life:
   _____
   _____

2. The Scripture passage that spoke to me with the most meaning (write the Scripture or your paraphrase of it):
   _____
   _____
   _____

3. One thing I need to confess to the Lord and ask forgiveness for:
   _____

4. One thing I need to praise the Lord for:
   _____

5. One important change the Lord and I need to make in my life:
   _____

6. The next step I need to take in obedience:
   _____

The Season of Renewal

WEEK 3

RESTORATION

On a Thanksgiving Day in the early 1970s, my family experienced a touching moment. My brother, Robert, had just returned home from Vietnam. Our family had survived the Vietnam era intact. Not everyone's family could say the same.

As we sat down to Thanksgiving dinner, we bowed our heads, and my father began to pray. "Lord," he said, "I just want to say thank You…" At that point he choked up and couldn't finish his prayer. He excused himself from the table. It was the first time I had ever seen him cry. The rest of us got all choked up too.

When he returned a few minutes later, I asked my father, "What was that all about?"

"I'm just so happy. You see, your mother and I didn't think we would ever see the family all together again."

No joy could ever exceed that of a father who sees his child return safely after a long absence.

God experiences that same joy when one of His children returns to close fellowship and communion with Him. Restoration begins with repentance and confession of sin. Nothing you do can earn your way to the Father. Only confession and repentance can open the door to God's loving forgiveness.

In the next four weeks, we will consider the following issues related to the Season of Renewal:

- The story of the prodigal son can be your story.
- Your relationship with Christ is the foundation for your identity.
- In the long run, serving God must overflow from a relationship with God.
- *Defining moments* in your life are opportunities for God to shape your life and calling.

The man who abandons God to pursue his own plans will not be abandoned by God. When our plans lead in a wrong direction, God will send reversals into our lives to humble us and turn our hearts back to Him. The man who has suffered *reversals* due to *rebellion* can experience *restoration* through *repentance*.

During your study this first week, you will:
- Understand the stages of restoration.
- Learn about the infinite grace of God.
- Discover the hope that you can break out of a downward spiral through the grace of God.

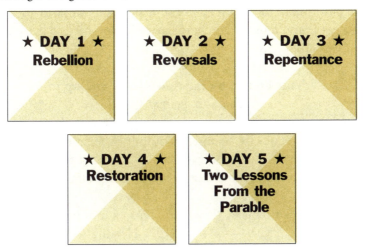

Memorize and meditate on this Scripture passage each day:

"If we confess our sins, he [God] is faithful and just and will forgive us our sins and purify us from all unrighteousness" (1 John 1:9).

Claim that reality for yourself this week. There is no better time to confess and no gift greater than eternal life.

DAY 1

REBELLION

Ask, "How many years after you received Christ did you really start to do business with God?" and the majority of men in a typical group won't respond until you suggest 8, 9, or 10 years. There seems to be a pattern for men to receive Christ, and then live a number of years without the full impact of His presence and power at work in their lives. They accept Jesus Christ as Lord and Savior but proceed to live out their own dreams and plans.

◆

Men who live by their own ideas end up in rebellion against God.

Many times this is not by a sinister plot, but by simple neglect of their relationship with their Heavenly Father. When men move away from their Father, their relationship begins to wane and diminish.

I once heard a man remark, "If you are sensing a distance in your relationship with God, guess who's moved?" Hearing God's voice clearly and often depends on us moving closer to God. In James 4:8 we read, "Come near to God and he will come near to you."

The story of the prodigal son shows how a man can suffer *reversals* because of his *rebellion*, yet experience *restoration* through *repentance*. By studying the four stages this young man went through, we can better understand how God longs to restore us.

Are you living in close fellowship with your Heavenly Father? Or are you a prodigal son? Put an x on the line that represents how close you are to God right now.

Distant from God						Close to God
Struggling to hear God						Hearing God's voice

WEEK 3, RESTORATION

Stale relationship with God   Fresh relationship with God

Bored with God   Excited about growing with God

Now, let's review the story of the prodigal son.

"Jesus continued: 'There was a man who had two sons. The younger one said to his father, "Father, give me my share of the estate." So he divided his property between them. Not long after that, the younger son got together all he had, set off for a distant country and there squandered his wealth in wild living'" (Luke 15:11-13).

The younger son decided to put some distance between himself and his father. This moving away is **rebellion.** In this story, we can detect four ways a man rebels against the Father.

1. Impatience with God's timing. God's timing does not always coincide with our desires. Let's be candid. The more power we possess to *not* wait, the harder it is to wait and to allow God to work out the details of our situations in His way and in His time. If you have the ability to reason through a problem, why shouldn't you go ahead? The son could not wait for his father to distribute the inheritance. He wanted what was his NOW! *Taking action before we sense God leading us signifies rebellion.*

🖌 How are you handling God's timing in your life? How is your patience index? (Circle one.)

    High   Above Average   OK   Low   Nonexistent

🖌 Here are three selected passages from the Psalms. Read each one and circle a word or phrase that describes how we are to wait on God.

"In the morning, Lord, you hear my voice; in the morning I lay my requests before you and wait in expectation" (Psalm 5:3).

"Wait for the Lord; be strong and take heart and wait for the Lord" (Psalm 27:14).

We wait in hope for the Lord; he is our help and our shield" (Psalm 33:20).

What do those verses mean for you specifically?

_____

2. Desire to be in control. The son wanted complete independence from his father. We may run away from our Father, like the prodigal son. But with all our debts and duties, when we rebel, it's more likely we'll stay where we are. Like a disgruntled employee who cripples productivity, we drag our feet in protest. We want control and pout when we don't get it. Or we don't want to trouble God where we are strong, so we don't consult Him in prayer or read the Bible for guidance.

Who controls each aspect of your life? Check one box on each line to indicate where you are right now.

God is in control ❏   ❏ I'm running things
I'm strong and don't need God ❏   ❏ I'm weak and need God

3. Financial irresponsibility. The son squandered his wealth in a distant country on new friends who were there only as long as the money flowed. Financial irresponsibility is a form of rebellion against God.

Here are some signs of modern financial irresponsibility. Check any that apply to you.
- ❏ Not saving
- ❏ Accumulating debt
- ❏ Spending more than earning
- ❏ Buying impulsively

4. Moral lapse or decline. The son wasted his money on wild living, parties, and prostitutes. Few men today plunge so quickly into moral decadence, but they slowly and subtly slide into a state of moral decline by a thousand small choices strung out over the years, none of which by themselves seem to matter much.

WEEK 3, RESTORATION

🖌 Examine your moral life. Have you experienced any of the following recently?
- ❏ Read a pornographic magazine or viewed a sexually-explicit movie.
- ❏ Fantasized about sex with another woman.
- ❏ Looked lustfully at another woman.
- ❏ Listened to or told off-color jokes.
- ❏ Talked loosely or crudely about sex.

Listen to what God's Word says you need to be doing.

"The weapons we fight with are not the weapons of the world. On the contrary, they have divine power to demolish strongholds. We demolish arguments and every pretension that sets itself up against the knowledge of God, and we take captive every thought to make it obedient to Christ. (2 Corinthians 10:4-5).

🖌 In closing today's study, select from the following the prayer(s) you need to pray right now. Silently offer your prayer to God.
- ❏ Lord Jesus, grant me patience to wait on You.
- ❏ Lord Jesus, I surrender complete control of my life to You.
- ❏ Lord Jesus, I need Your help and wisdom in my finances.
- ❏ Lord Jesus, I need Your power to take every thought captive and to keep my moral life pure.

The Bottom Line
- Men who live by their own ideas end up in rebellion against God.
- Taking action before we sense God leading us signifies rebellion.
- Financial irresponsibility and moral lapse and decline are forms of rebellion against God.

DAY 2

REVERSALS

"After he had spent everything, there was a severe famine in that whole country, and he began to be in need. So he went and hired himself out to a citizen of that country, who sent him to his fields to feed pigs. He longed to fill his stomach with the pods that the pigs were eating, but no one gave him anything" (Luke 15:14-16).

The son blew his bankroll and—notice that only after it was gone—then comes the famine. "After he had spent everything, there was a severe famine in that whole country." Isn't that the way life goes? The contingency doesn't strike until the contingency fund is depleted!

◆

**After a rebellious spirit has run its course,
a reversal grabs our attention.**

God sends a famine! Why did God wait until the son had spent all? Perhaps God wanted to make sure the young man had no vestige of his own resources left upon which he could fall back and prolong his rebellion against his father.

The key phrase in this passage is, "He began to be in need." When all is going well, it's often hard for us to recognize our need for God. Jesus strongly warns the rich, not because riches are wrong, but because the rich often become insensitive to their need for God and the needs of others.

When we find ourselves in a destructive cycle in life, why do we refuse to turn to God before we hit bottom? Why didn't the prodigal son just go home? Perhaps he was embarrassed to have been such a fool. Maybe it was pride. Possibly he was blinded by self-deceit. Or could he have been in a state of depression? More to the point, why don't you and I turn back after we start to be in want? When our sins, like those of the prodigal son, blind us, we often turn to everyone but God.

🖌 When you find yourself in a destructive cycle of rebellion, what keeps you from turning back to the loving Father and asking forgiveness? (Check all that apply to you.)
- ❏ My pride.
- ❏ My belief that I can turn things around by myself.
- ❏ My depression keeps me from doing anything.
- ❏ My desire to show God I'm in control.
- ❏ My self-deceit that I'm really OK when I'm not.
- ❏ Other: _____

To add insult to injury, when the prodigal son faced famine, no one would give him anything. What happened to all those "friends" who helped him squander his father's fortune?

🖌 Have you ever been through a period of reversals, gone to your friends for help, but no one would lend a hand? Describe that time.

_____

_____

Scripture tells us, "A friend loves at all times, and a brother is born for adversity." It also says, "A man of many companions may come to ruin, but there is a friend who sticks closer than a brother" (Proverbs 17:17, 18:24). For the prodigal son, and for us as well, that friend was the patient and forgiving Father.

Our response to reversals in life is critical. We have two choices. We can harden our hearts toward God, blaming Him and others for our problems; or, we can see reversals as an opportunity to throw ourselves completely on the mercies and resources of our loving Father.

No man ever reaches such great spiritual maturity that he doesn't need God in his life. Neither does any man plunge to such great depth of depravity that God gives up on him.

THE SEASONS OF CRISIS AND RENEWAL

🖌 Are you facing reversals in your life? Don't harden your heart. Listen to the promises of your loving Father. Read the following passages and underline key words or phrases that speak to your circumstances.

"I can do everything through him who gives me strength" (Philippians 4:13).

"If my people, who are called by my name, will humble themselves and pray and seek my face and turn from their wicked ways, then will I hear from heaven and will forgive their sin and will heal their land" (2 Chronicles 7:14).

"Submit yourselves, then, to God. Resist the devil, and he will flee from you. Come near to God and he will come near you. Wash your hands, you sinners, and purify your hearts, you double-minded. Grieve, mourn and wail. Change your laughter to mourning and your joy to gloom. Humble yourselves before the Lord, and he will lift you up" (James 4:7-10).

🖌 In closing today, pray this simple prayer.

Lord Jesus, I cannot change 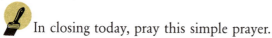 my circumstances. I cannot turn things around or change myself. Lord, forgive me, change me, and make me a new creation through the power of your Holy Spirit. Amen.

The Bottom Line
- After a rebellious spirit has run its course, a reversal grabs our attention.
- The contingency doesn't strike until the contingency fund is depleted!
- When all is going well, it's often hard for us to recognize our need for God.

DAY 3

REPENTANCE

After a man rebels against God, he inevitably faces reversals in his life.

◆

Reversals will either lead you to run further *from* God or run from sin *to* God.

"When he came to his senses, he said, 'How many of my father's hired men have food to spare, and here I am starving to death! I will set out and go back to my father and say to him: Father, I have sinned against heaven and against you. I am no longer worthy to be called your son; make me like one of your hired men.' So he got up and went to his father" (Luke 15:17-20).

At this point we have a full-blown crisis. *Rebellion* has led to *reversals*. In the depths of his despair, this young man came to his senses and turned toward home.

A self-made crisis will drive us to our knees for a time of self-examination. A crisis is a gift from God that points us back toward Him. It is a gift because God does not let us destroy ourselves. Our deep miseries invite us to return to the unfailing love of our perfect Father.

Repentance means to turn away from sin and back to God. Read again Luke 15:17-20. Match the list of things he turned from and then toward by drawing a line between them.

1. He turned from confusion to
2. He turned from denying reality to
3. He turned from rebellion to
4. He turned from a foreign land to

- confession
- home
- clarity (good sense)
- truth

Let's look closer at each of these components of repentance.

1. Confusion to clarity. Rebellion leaves us in a confused state of mind. The enemy, the world, and our own thinking flood us with confusion. Then we are unable to discern God's will, plan, and direction for our lives. When you are confused, what works best for you?

THE SEASONS OF CRISIS AND RENEWAL

🖌 Below is a list of ways to dispel confusion. Prioritize which steps are most effective in your spiritual life.
  _____ Reading God's Word.
  _____ Being counseled by a Christian friend.
  _____ Worshiping and praising God.
  _____ Prayer.
  _____ Talking with my pastor.
  _____ Other:_____

No one way will be adequate by itself to see God clearly. It's a combination of ways which helps us move from confusion to clarity.

2. Denial to truth. As we come to our senses, we admit the truth about ourselves and our circumstances. We leave behind our state of denial. The unreformed alcoholic denies he has a problem. The abuser denies his abusive behavior. The addict denies he's addicted. All sinners must turn from denial to the truth.

The truth for the prodigal son was simple: "Here I am starving to death!" Coming face-to-face with reality helps break the bondage and blindness of sin. Accepting the truth sets us free.

🖌 Read John 8:32 and write a paraphrase applying the passage to your circumstances.
"Then you will know the truth, and the truth will set you free."

---

3. Rebellion to confession. Repentance means we turn from rebellion to a loving Father. The lie of rebellion is that God has stopped loving you. The enemy deceives you into believing God will never forgive you. What you've done is too terrible and God will not have you back.

🖌 Here are just a few truths about God's love for you. Fill in the blanks using the following words: first, sinners, everlasting, mercy, Son.
  God loves us with an _____ love (Jeremiah 31:3).
  We love because he _____ loved us (1 John 4:19).
  God loves us so much he gave His _____ (John 3:16).

WEEK 3, RESTORATION

In His love for us, God is rich in _____ (Ephesians 2:4).
God demonstrates his love for us in that while we are still _____,
Christ died for us (Romans 5:8).

In the depth of his despair, it dawned on the prodigal son that he would be far better off with his father, even if only as a hired hand. He felt so unworthy to be called a son, a sure sign of contrition and repentance. Meanwhile, the father was longing for his son to return even while the son was rebelling in a far country.

4. Foreign land to home. The son turned from the foreign land of sin, rebellion, and death, and set his course toward home. Jesus invites us to come home to the Father (see John 14).

Honestly answer the following questions.

Have you done something that has separated you from the Father?	❑ Yes	❑ No
If so, have you come to your senses?	❑ Yes	❑ No
Do you need to repent?	❑ Yes	❑ No
Will you come home to the Father?	❑ Yes	❑ No

If there is unconfessed sin in your life right now, don't wait. Stop carrying around the baggage of guilt. Ask the Lord's forgiveness. Close in prayer to God.

The Bottom Line
- Reversals will either lead you to run further *from* God or run from sin *to* God.
- A crisis is a gift from God that points us back toward Him.
- *Repentance* means to turn away from sin and back to God.

DAY 4

RESTORATION

Now we come to the joyful part of the prodigal son's story. Read it and celebrate!

> So he got up and went to his father.
>
> But while he was still a long way off, his father saw him and was filled with compassion for him; he ran to his son, threw his arms around him and kissed him.
>
> The son said to him, "Father, I have sinned against heaven and against you. I am no longer worthy to be called your son."
>
> But the father said to his servants, "Quick! Bring the best robe and put it on him. Put a ring on his finger and sandals on his feet. Bring the fattened calf and kill it. Let's have a feast and celebrate. For this son of mine was dead and is alive again; he was lost and is found." So they began to celebrate (Luke 15:20-24).

If we subtitled Day 3, "What the Son Did," we would then subtitle Day 4, "What the Father Did."

 List all the things the Father did to restore his son.

_____

_____

The father did two things. First, the father lavished his son with love. He had compassion for his son. The Greek word for compassion means "to have the bowels yearn, to feel sympathy, and to have pity." This father actually ran to meet his son, threw his arms around him, and kissed him.

Second, the father restored the son. When the son tendered the repentance speech he had been rehearsing, that was all the father needed.

It's ironic. While the son felt remorse, the father felt joy. Actually *because* the son felt remorse, the father felt joy. God and His angels rejoice when we repent (see Luke 15:10).

WEEK 3, RESTORATION

◆

When we return to God, He restores us and lavishes us with love.

We have identified the components of restoration:
Rebellion → Reversals → Repentance → Restoration

Our Heavenly Father always seeks complete restoration in our relationship with Him. The biblical word for that is *reconciliation*. Second Corinthians 5:19 declares, "God was reconciling the world to himself in Christ, not counting men's sins against them."

What keeps us from being fully reconciled and restored to God? Certainly Christ has done it all—He died for us on the cross. If anything hinders us from being restored fully, it's our own doubts and fears.

Check anything below that keeps you from reaching out to God.
- ❏ "I'll be rejected."
- ❏ "Oh, what guilt I feel."
- ❏ "God won't forgive me."
- ❏ "I can't admit I'm wrong."
- ❏ "I don't deserve forgiveness."
- ❏ "What I've done is too terrible to be forgiven."
- ❏ "Others will put me down and accuse me."
- ❏ Other: _____

Restoration is not based on feelings. You may feel unforgiven and guilty. You may feel unworthy and rejected.

Scripture tells us we are to wrestle with our sin and conform our actions and attitudes to Christ's example. Then it adds, "This then is how we know that we belong to the truth, and how we set our hearts at rest in his presence whenever our hearts condemn us. For God is greater than our hearts, and he knows everything" (1 John 3:19-20).

According to that passage, after you've repented and changed your behavior, who are you to trust regarding your standing before God?
❏ Your heart   ❏ God and His Word

If we continue to feel guilt, it's not because we have to. The verse highlighted in this week's introduction, 1 John 1:9, states clearly that true confession and repentance always brings God's forgiveness.

But we must be careful that we don't continue to sin intentionally, thus taking advantage of God's grace. The price of restoration and reconciliation is the shed blood of Jesus Christ. The clearer we see the cross, the more we desire to come home to the Father.

Below is the description from Isaiah of Jesus' dying for our sins. Read it slowly, carefully, and out loud. Underline the ways Jesus suffered for our sin. Circle the ways Jesus cleanses us from sin.

> Who has believed our message
> > and to whom has the arm of the Lord been revealed?
> He grew up before him like a tender shoot,
> > and like a root out of dry ground.
> He had no beauty or majesty to attract us to him,
> > nothing in his appearance that we should desire him.
> He was despised and rejected by men,
> > a man of sorrows, and familiar with suffering.
> Like one from whom men hide their faces
> > he was despised, and we esteemed him not.
>
> Surely he took up our infirmities
> > and carried our sorrows,
> yet we considered him stricken by God,
> > smitten by him, and afflicted.
> But he was pierced for our transgressions,
> > he was crushed for our iniquities;
> the punishment that brought us peace was upon him,
> > and by his wounds we are healed.
> We all, like sheep, have gone astray,
> > each of us has turned to his own way;
> and the Lord has laid on him
> > the iniquity of us all.
> He was oppressed and afflicted,
> > yet he did not open his mouth;
> he was led like a lamb to the slaughter,
> > and as a sheep before her shearers is silent,
> > so he did not open his mouth.

By oppression and judgment he was taken away.
    And who can speak of his descendants?
For he was cut off from the land of the living;
    for the transgression of my people he was stricken.
He was assigned a grave with the wicked,
    and with the rich in his death,
though he had done no violence,
    nor was any deceit in his mouth.

Yet it was the Lord's will to crush him and
      cause him to suffer,
    and though the Lord makes his life a guilt offering,
he will see his offspring and prolong his days,
    and the will of the Lord will prosper in his hand.
After the suffering of his soul,
    he will see the light [of life] and be satisfied;
by his knowledge my righteous servant will justify many,
    and he will bear their iniquities.
Therefore I will give him a portion among the great,
    and he will divide the spoils with the strong,
because he poured out his life unto death,
    and was numbered with the transgressors.
For he bore the sin of many,
    and made intercession for the transgressors (Isaiah 53).

In closing today, give thanks for restoration through Jesus' sacrifice.

The Bottom Line
- When we return to God, He restores us and lavishes us with love.
- Because the son felt remorse, the father felt joy.
- Christ has provided everything for our reconciliation to God.
- Restoration is not based on our feelings, but on God's Word.

DAY 5

TWO LESSONS FROM THE PARABLE

The parable of the loving father and prodigal son teaches us two lessons.

1. No sin is so terrible that God will not forgive you. No matter how far away from God you have been living, you can find your way back. If a young man who rejected his father's values, took half his father's wealth, debased himself in immoral living, and lost all his fortune on wild living can be restored to his father, so can we be restored to our heavenly Father through repentance.

◆

God comes running to meet us when we turn to Him in our hearts.

Listed below are some great men of God in Scripture and a text that reveals one of their sins. Match names with the sin God forgave.

Mighty Man of God	Sin(s)
Abraham (Genesis 12:10-20)	• Killed an officer so he could take the officer's wife for his own.
Aaron (Numbers 12)	• Misrepresented God to the Israelites.
Moses (Numbers 20:12-13)	• Shared the secret of his power.
Samson (Judges 16)	• Persecuted followers of the Way.
David (2 Samuel 11)	• Lied about his wife Sarai.
Peter (Matthew 26:69-74)	• Spread false rumors about Moses.
Paul/Saul (Acts 9:1-2)	• Denied knowing Christ.

God does not take sin lightly. His Son died for our sins. But God's love provides us a way to Him through the cross.

WEEK 3, RESTORATION

🖌 Psalm 103:2-5 shows us the type of love that God has for His children. When we ask God to forgive our sins, He does it with gladness and joy. Read this personalized version of this Psalm as a prayer to God.

> Praise the Lord, O my soul,
>   and forget not all his benefits—
> who forgives all [my] sins
>   and heals all [my] diseases,
> who redeems [my] life from the pit
>   and crowns [my] with love and compassion,
> who satisfies [my] desires with good things
> so that [my] youth is renewed like the eagle's.

2. You can break out of the downward spiral into crisis at any point. A full-blown rebellion means crisis, but full-blown repentance means restoration. Immediate repentance brings immediate forgiveness. You may reap the consequences of your sin for some time to come. But in the midst of future difficulties, God will restore, love, and forgive you. No longer does the punishment and guilt of your sin hang over you. David tells us of a wonderful promise.

> For as high as the heavens are above the earth,
>   so great is his love for those who fear him;
> as far as the east is from the west,
>   so far has he removed our transgressions from us
> (Psalm 103:11-12).

If you have been suffering through a crisis of your own making and want to be reunited with your heavenly Father, you can do so right now through prayer. Express your desire, your remorse for sinning against God, your sorrow for hurting those you love the most, your sense of unworthiness to even be called His son, your pledge to change directions, and your willingness to be a servant.

THE SEASONS OF CRISIS AND RENEWAL

Pray this suggested prayer, paraphrase it, or use it as a guide to make up your own. Pray and allow God to begin restoring you.

> *Lord Jesus and Father God, I am perishing from hunger for You. My circumstances are in shambles. Against You, O God, have I sinned. I despise my sins and repent of my rebellion against You. Forgive me, Lord, according to Your great mercy. Forgive me for the pain I have caused my loved ones, and show me how to restore those relationships. I am unworthy to even be called Your son. By Your grace, restore me to wholeness. Restore me to a right relationship with You and a right relationship with the people in my life. I surrender control of my life to You. I make a pledge of new obedience. Make me into Your servant. Amen.*

The Bottom Line
- No matter how far away from God you have been living, you can find your way back.
- God comes running to meet us when we turn to Him in our hearts.
- A full-blown rebellion means crisis, but full-blown repentance means restoration.
- No longer does the punishment and guilt of your sin hang over you; God will restore, love, and forgive you.

 This week you discovered …
- the stages of restoration: rebellion, reversals, repentance, restoration.
- how you can receive God's grace and break out of the downward spiral of crisis.

What does God want you to do in response to this week's study?

Recite 1 John 1:9 as a closing thought for the week.

WEEK 4

A NEW MESSAGE FOR MEN

Francis Schaeffer wrote that life is like a house with two stories. The first holds the lower order of man, earth, and created things. The second story contains God, heaven, and eternal things.[1] God intends for the new man in Jesus Christ to live and move in both stories. Scripture says it this way:

> Since, then, you have been raised with Christ, set your hearts on things above, where Christ is seated at the right hand of God. Set your minds on things above, not on earthly things. For you died, and your life is now hidden with Christ in God (Colossians 3:1-3).
>
> [From now on] those who use the things of the world, [should live] as if not engrossed in them. For this world in its present form is passing away (1 Corinthians 7:31).

This week you will discover:
- Second-story versus first-story living;
- *Whose* you are instead of *who* you are;
- *Who* is your purpose instead of *what* is your purpose; and,
- The importance of knowing and loving God more deeply.

THE SEASONS OF CRISIS AND RENEWAL

★ **DAY 1** ★
The Two-Story Kingdom

★ **DAY 2** ★
Who Am I?
-vs-
Whose Am I?

★ **DAY 3** ★
What-vs-*Who*
Is the Purpose of My Life?

★ **DAY 4** ★
An Organizing Principle

★ **DAY 5** ★
The Challenge to Change Paradigms

As you study, read the Scriptures for each lesson and carefully complete the exercises. You will begin to discover how God works in your life during the Season of Renewal.

Memorize and meditate on this Scripture passage each day.

"Since, then, you have been raised with Christ, set your hearts on things above, where Christ is seated at the right hand of God. Set your minds on things above, not on earthly things. For you died, and your life is now hidden with Christ in God" (Colossians 3:1-3).

I pray that this week you will move toward renewal in your life through God's power and Spirit.

---

[1] Francis A. Schaeffer, *Escape from Reason* (Downer's Grove: InterVarsity Press, 1968), 9.

DAY 1

THE TWO-STORY KINGDOM

In the introduction, I explained Francis Shaeffer's concept that life is like a house with two stories. The first holds the things of this life. The second holds the things of eternity. The problem, then, is that for several decades we have been falling down the stairs into a Christian culture preoccupied with first-story issues—issues centered on this life and man.

We have believed the self-help gospel of Cultural Christianity that never rises above the first floor. It teaches us to be good instead of sanctified. The goals of being a better husband and dad, managing time better, making better decisions, becoming a better money manager, and being successful are important, but they represent an anemic victory if we neglect the greater second-story demands of authentic faith.

This Cultural Christianity often focuses on how to become successful enough to distance ourselves from the troubles of other people rather than on how to take the Bread of Life to people starving to spiritual death. We insulate ourselves from the aches and pains of a world held hostage to sin. We can yearn to live in a gated community that holds at bay the woes of the world. We end up preaching to ourselves "the gospel of the gated community."

Below is a list of genuine second-story concerns of the kingdom of God and a text where they may be found. Check how often you have been involved in each.

1. Sharing Christ and the Gospel with someone (Matthew 28:19-20).
   ❏ Often ❏ Sometimes ❏ Never
2. Visiting the sick (Matthew 25:36).
   ❏ Often ❏ Sometimes ❏ Never
3. Using your spiritual gifts (Romans 12:4-16).
   ❏ Often ❏ Sometimes ❏ Never
4. Praying for others (James 5:13-20).
   ❏ Often ❏ Sometimes ❏ Never
5. Giving to the poor (Acts 20:35).
   ❏ Often ❏ Sometimes ❏ Never

6. Being a true Christian friend (Galatians 6:2).
   ❏ Often ❏ Sometimes ❏ Never
7. Giving cheerfully to the work of the Lord (2 Corinthians 9).
   ❏ Often ❏ Sometimes ❏ Never
8. Keeping your love relationship with God (Luke 10:25-27).
   ❏ Often ❏ Sometimes ❏ Never

Here is the core problem for men:

◆

The mainly economic man is not a whole man.

There is no sustaining passion, no fire in the belly, of a man preoccupied only with issues of the first story. When we concentrate our energy exclusively on building a better life for ourselves, we put a ceiling on how much our lives can count.

Authentic satisfaction, a life that counts, a life that matters, a life that makes a difference—these we find only in the second story. The power of God is in the second story.

 How much of your life are you living in the second story?

No significant   Strong second-
second-story activity   story activity

What keeps you from climbing the stairs to the second story?

Some Drawbacks

I don't know how you answered the previous question, but I do know two general barricades that keep men stuck on the first floor. First, to be a successful man in today's economic climate demands a great deal of concentration. In the pressure cooker of commerce, men forget to worship their Creator. Men become so busy, they lose sight of their larger purpose. Are you too busy for God?

Second, in many cases the culture has influenced the church more than the church has influenced the culture. Consequently, much preaching doesn't lift the spirits of men into the heavenlies. Rather, the focus remains earthbound. When men go to church, what they want, whether they can express it or not, is to hear a word from the Lord, to be brought into the presence of the living God through authentic worship, music, confessions, creeds, and preaching of God's Word. Too often they never got out of the first story.

How are you experiencing God? Circle the words that best describe your spiritual life.

Inspiring	Uplifting	Boring	Draining	Empowering
Exciting	Joyful	Dutiful	Anxious	Dynamic
Authentic	Plastic	Hypocritical	Real	Detached
Depressing	Miraculous	Entertaining	Holy	Meaningful

A New Message for Men
God has a message for men stuck in the first story: "I love you, but you cannot be a Christian on your own terms." I believe the Lord wants us to move fully into the second story without abandoning the first.

God invites you to join Him in the second story. In your own Bible, read Colossians 3:1-4. Summarize the main idea of these verses.

___

Now read Colossians 3:5-17. How do these attitudes and actions relate to the idea of verses 1-4? Why does Paul say *therefore*?

___

THE SEASONS OF CRISIS AND RENEWAL

 What does God want you to do as a result of today's study?

_____

_____

In closing, pray this prayer:

Lord, Jesus, fill me with Your Holy Spirit that I might live fully in Your kingdom, not the kingdom I build. Help me move fully into the second story without abandoning the first story. Help me make You the central focus of my heart. Amen.

The Bottom Line
- Met goals represent an anemic victory if we neglect the greater second story demands of authentic faith.
- The mainly economic man is not a whole man.
- Authentic satisfaction, a life that counts, a life that matters, a life that makes a difference—these we find only in the second story.
- The Lord wants us to move fully into the second story without abandoning the first.

DAY 2

Who Am I? -vs- *Whose Am I?*

For the last several years I have encouraged men to ask the questions, "Who am I?" and "What is the purpose of my life?" I have also suggested men write out a Written Life-Purpose Statement to reflect their understanding of the answers they get to these questions. These are issues of identity, meaning, and purpose. They are critical questions. They are, and always will be, good questions.

I have come to see how we can make ourselves earth-bound and culture-bound by them. Although we should keep asking them, I have come to believe they have a man-centered (anthropocentric) thrust rather than a God-centered (theocentric) focus. They belong to the first story. However, by massaging the questions a bit, we can create an additional pair of questions that will bring us upstairs into the second story.

Before we can successfully know, "*Who* am I?" we must first know, "*Whose* am I?" To correctly know, "*What* is the purpose of my life?" we must first know "*Who* is the purpose of my life?"

When we change the nuance of these questions, we force them upstairs into the second story. We shift the focus to God.

The Bible declares that we are created in the image of God. Read the following Scriptures and summarize in two sentences what they say about God's purpose and design for us.

"Then God said, 'Let us make man in our image, in our likeness, and let them rule over the fish of the sea and the birds of the air, over the livestock, over all the earth, and over all the creatures that move along the ground.'

So God created man in his own image" (Genesis 1:26-27).

"When I consider your heavens, the work of your fingers, the moon and the stars, which you have set in place, what is man that you are mindful of him, the son of man that you care for him? You made him a little lower than the heavenly beings and crowned him with glory and honor. You made him ruler over the works of your hands" (Psalm 8:3-6).

THE SEASONS OF CRISIS AND RENEWAL

"'For in him [God] we live and move and have our being.' As some of your own poets have said, 'We are his offspring'" (Acts 17:28).

_____

_____

You represent God's crowning achievement. You are His most excellent creation. You are the full expression of God's creative genius. You were created to be in relationship with Him.

The question "Who am I?" deals with our identity. The question "*Whose* am I?" deals with our identity *in relation to our Creator*. To know ourselves, we must also know something of the nature and character of the One who made us—what is His design, plan, and purpose for mankind?

◆

The most important part of knowing *who* you are is knowing *whose* you are.

Summarize how the following Scriptures reveal *whose* we are.

Text	In Christ We ...
"Do you not know that your body is a temple of the Holy Spirit, who is in you, whom you have received from God? You are not your own; you were bought at a price. Therefore honor God with your body" (1 Corinthians 6:19-20).	_____
"And he [Jesus] died for all, that those who live should no longer live for themselves but for him who died for them and was raised again" (2 Corinthians 5:15).	_____
"I have been crucified with Christ and I no longer live, but Christ lives in me" (Galatians 2:20).	_____

WEEK 4, A NEW MESSAGE FOR MEN

"For to me, to live is Christ and to die is gain" (Philippians 1:21).

"Once you were not a people, but now you are the people of God; once you had not received mercy, but now you have received mercy" (1 Peter 2:10).

What should a man say in response to all this? Perhaps something like this: "I am who I am because of the grace of God. He has made me. I belong to Jesus. I am not my own; I have been bought with a price. I am a slave of Jesus Christ. I should no longer (and by God's conquering grace will no longer) live for myself but for Him who died for me and was raised again. I have been crucified with Christ, and I no longer live. The life I live in the body I live by faith in Him who loved me and gave Himself for me. For me, to live is Christ; to die is gain. Whatever was to my profit I now consider loss for the sake of Christ."

We are who we are because of Whose we are. Based on your relationship with Jesus Christ, close today's study by writing a description of who you are in Jesus Christ.

In Jesus Christ, I, _____ , am _____
(your name)

The Bottom Line
- The Bible declares that we are created in the image of God.
- You were created to be in relationship with Him.
- The most important part of knowing *who* you are is knowing *whose* you are.

DAY 3

WHAT -VS-*WHO* IS THE PURPOSE OF MY LIFE

Most men I know would prefer to "do" something for God rather than simply "be" with Him. This task-oriented approach to Christian faith can lead to a huge spiritual defeat.

How we ask about the purpose of our lives reveals our focus. For example, "What is my purpose?" points us to the task God has for my life. Certainly there is work to be done as a Christian. On the other hand, we need to ask, *"Who is the purpose of my life?"* This question focuses on my *relationship* with Christ.

🖌 The beginning of the book of Revelation records Jesus' letters to seven churches, the first being the church at Ephesus. Look up that passage in Revelation 2:1-7.

What did Jesus commend this church for in verse 2?

_____

What did He condemn this church for in verse 4?

_____

You will see this same characteristic in the prodigal son's older brother. We concluded last week's study with the father's celebration at the return of his wandering son. But that's not the end of the story.

According to Jesus' parable, the older son was working in the fields when his younger brother came home. When he heard the sounds of celebration, he became angry and refused to go inside. This is how he answered his father's pleading, " 'Look! All these years I've been slaving for you and never disobeyed your orders. Yet you never gave me even a young goat so I could celebrate with my friends' " (Luke 15:29).

🖌 Where was he finding his purpose and sense of self-worth?
  ❑ tasks performed   ❑ relationship with the father

The father replied, "My son, you are always with me, and everything I have is yours" (Luke 15:31). Then he explained why he was celebrating the younger son's return.

On what was he basing his older son's worth?
❑ tasks performed   ❑ relationship with the father

The point is simple, yet profound. God created us to be human "beings" not human "doings."

◆

We cannot correctly answer the question "*What* is the purpose of my life?" until we correctly answer the question "*Who* is the purpose for my life?"

The relationship between Jesus and His Heavenly Father perfectly illustrates this principle. Jesus describes His relationship with the Father throughout the Gospel of John. Underline everything that points to the relationship Jesus has with the Father.

"When you have lifted up the Son of Man, then you will know that I am the one I claim to be and that I do nothing on my own but speak just what the Father has taught me. The one who sent me is with me; he has not left me alone, for I always do what pleases Him" (John 8:28-29). Notice Jesus' focus is on His relationship with God, not what He is doing for God, likewise, out of a relationship with Jesus Christ flows life and all the fruit we bear. Without that relationship, our lives can bear no good fruit. Listen closely to what Jesus says: "I am the vine; you are the branches. If a man remains in me and I in him, he will bear much fruit; apart from me you can do nothing" (John 15:5).

Put an x on each line at the place that represents where you are in your relationship with Christ.

Listening to others					Listening to Him
Seeking a purpose					Seeking Him
Wondering who I am					Knowing Whose I am

Please don't misunderstand what's being taught here. Serving Jesus Christ is important. It's just not the most important thing. Serving God is best when it comes from gratitude for knowing God. If we don't focus on *who* is the purpose of our lives, *what* we do won't have much meaning.

Review today's lesson. What one statement or Scripture had the most meaning for you? Write it below.

_____

_____

What does God want you to do as a result of today's study?

_____

_____

In closing, sit silently. Tell Christ how much you love and adore Him. Pray this prayer: "Father, I adore You. Jesus, I love You. Holy Spirit, You are welcome in my heart. Amen."

> **The Bottom Line**
> - Most men would prefer to "do" something for God rather than simply "be" with Him.
> - A task-oriented approach to Christian faith can lead to a huge spiritual defeat.
> - We cannot correctly answer the question "*What* is the purpose for my life?" until we correctly answer the question "*Who* is the purpose for my life?"

DAY 4

AN ORGANIZING PRINCIPLE

In 1991, I gave up day-to-day business responsibilities to devote more time to a calling I received in 1988 "to take God's message of love to a broken generation," and to the vision of "helping to bring about a spiritual awakening in America by reaching men and leaders of our nation with Christ."

These are noble purposes, but within weeks I found myself evaluating my performance by the same standards I had used in business. How many people attended my speeches? What percentage accepted Christ? How many books sold? Was it more than last month?

And I began to hate it. So I began praying for God to give me some sort of organizing principle around which I could order my life.

As I read *The Letters of Francis Schaeffer*, I wrote on my legal pad, "I will commit myself to a life of devotion and study of God, then speak, teach, and write about what I am learning."

Eureka! I thought. *That's it! The key to staying on track is a life of devotion and study of God.*

It's not just an important concept—it's the hinge on which everything else swings. Take some time to paraphrase it in a format you can apply to your own life.

_____

_____

_____

◆

Knowing and loving God should be the chief pursuit of every man's life.

THE SEASONS OF CRISIS AND RENEWAL

This organizing principle—however one might word it—has application for each of us. In other words, every man should be committed to a life of devotion and study of God. Then, after he is filled up to the overflow with enough Jesus for himself and some left over to give away to others, too, he should do whatever it is he is called to do—practice law or medicine, fix plumbing, sell, manage, mow lawns, drive a truck, perform accounting, or do whatever.

Now let's break down that principle into easy-to-understand pieces.

1. A life of devotion means to love God more and more.

How can we love God more and more? Loving God comes out of the overflow of a personal relationship with Him. Here are some ways to bring ourselves into closer communion with God. Check those that you would like to happen more in your life in the coming days.

- ❑ Talk with God in prayer.
- ❑ Listen to God's voice in Scripture.
- ❑ Participate in an organized Bible study.
- ❑ Tell others of my love for God.
- ❑ Praise God no matter what the circumstances.
- ❑ Tell God constantly of my love for Him.
- ❑ Journal and write down my love for God.
- ❑ Be still and share my heart with God.
- ❑ Allow the Holy Spirit to comfort, teach, and convict me.
- ❑ Be in an accountability group.
- ❑ Be actively involved in my church.

When I wrote my organizing principle, I realized that my relationship with God must always be a higher priority than the work I do for Him. A relationship takes time. You can delegate tasks but not relationships. No one can have a relationship with God for you. Your pastor, wife, and Christian friends cannot be intimate with God for you. Listening to them tell of their love for God never can replace loving God yourself.

We were made to have a vibrant relationship with God. Yet our sin causes us to desire a life of independence and indifference to Him. This kind of life can never satisfy. So we sometimes shuffle through our days with a vague sense that something is not quite right about our lives.

Jesus gives us the cure for our ills, "Love the Lord your God with all your heart and with all your soul and with all your mind" (Matthew 22:37). When we love God at the core of our being, He gives us a sense of meaning that overflows into every area of our lives.

2. A life of study means to know God more and more.

The Hebrew word for *know* means to be intimate with another person. The more clearly we know God, the more clearly we know who we should be. The brilliance of His character evaporates the fog that blankets our minds. The Bible says, "Now we see but a poor reflection as in a mirror; then we shall see face to face. Now I know in part; then I shall know fully, even as I am fully known" (1 Corinthians 13:12). The more we study, the more we know. The more we know, the more we will see God. The more we see God, the more we will become like Him.

God's goal is to bring us into an intimate relationship with Him. In the new heavens and new earth, we will love Him with all our hearts and we will know Him as He is. We will find ultimate fulfillment by loving, worshiping, and serving God.

So, it only makes sense that the key to staying on track now is a life of devotion and study of God. To love and to know God. These, then should become the chief pursuits of my life and yours, and everything else should proceed out of the overflow of a beautiful love relationship with God.

Write a prayer asking God to help you make that a reality in your life.

_____

_____

_____

_____

THE SEASONS OF CRISIS AND RENEWAL

Review today's lesson. What one statement was most meaningful to you? Write it below.

_____

_____

What does God want you to do as a result of today's study?

_____

_____

The Bottom Line
- Knowing and loving God should be the chief pursuits of every man's life.
- A life of devotion means to love God more and more.
- A man's relationship with God must always be a higher priority than the work he does for God.
- A life of study means to know God more and more.
- The key to staying on track now is a life of devotion and study of God.

DAY 5

THE CHALLENGE TO CHANGE PARADIGMS

We have been talking about the difference between Cultural Christianity and Biblical Christianity. Remember that in Cultural Christianity we are preoccupied with the first story of our lives. Biblical Christianity takes us to the second story, where God is. We are challenged to move from the visible to the invisible, from the natural to the supernatural.

◆

We must change paradigms in order to live in the second story.

Here is a contrast between Cultural Christianity and Biblical Christianity. Read this twice. The first time compare columns line by line. The second time read the whole column under each title.

Cultural Christianity	**Biblical Christianity**
Characteristics	*Characteristics*
First story only	Second story (without giving up the first)
Man, earth, things created	God, heaven, eternal things
"This world"-oriented	"Kingdom of God"-oriented
The God we want	The God who is
The gospel of the gated community	The gospel of the kingdom of heaven
A passive Christianity	An active Christianity
Goals/Emphasis	*Goals/Emphasis*
Self-help	Ushering in the kingdom
Personal fulfillment	Pleasing God
To be something	To be used by God
Guidance	God
Support	Salvation
Help	Holiness
My will	God's will
"Jesus belongs to me."	"I belong to Jesus."
Christ exists for man	Man exists for Christ

THE SEASONS OF CRISIS AND RENEWAL

Look over the first column. Circle those characteristics of Cultural Christianity with which you struggle most. Look over the second column. Circle first those qualities of Biblical Christianity that you are doing well with, then check those you need to develop.

What does it mean to follow Jesus completely and totally?
Read the following passages and write what it means to follow Jesus.

Jesus says...	I must...
"If anyone would come after me, he must deny himself and take up his cross and follow me" (Matthew 16:24).	
"My sheep listen to my voice; I know them, and they follow me" (John 10:27).	
"Whoever serves me must follow me; and where I am, my servant also will be. My Father will honor the one who serves me" (John 12:26).	

In 70 years the Communist ideology captured one-third of the earth's territory and population. The Communists understood a great principle: If you make a small challenge, you will get a small response. But if you present men with a great challenge, they will do something heroic.

It is interesting that today's churches that do present men with a strong challenge to live by the whole gospel—the gospel of the kingdom—have learned they will accept the challenge, and as a result, they are growing. Most men, after all, are heroes. Most men want to be "all the way" Christians, not "statistical" Christians—Biblical Christians and not Cultural Christians. They simply need someone to show them how.

I'm going to present you with a great challenge. I'm going to ask you to do something heroic, something that can turn the world upside "right"—something that will make your life count. If you have been living the life of a Cultural Christian, I'm going to ask you to become a Biblical Christian. Are you ready? If so, talk it over with Jesus. Pray in your own words, or you may wish to pray this prayer:

Lord Jesus, I surrender all to You. I desire to love and know You. I am tired of trying to be good enough for you to love me. I trust You completely. Save me. Forgive me. I desire to belong to You. I want Your purpose for my life. Take control of me. I die to self. I welcome the gift of Your Holy Spirit to indwell me. Thank You for giving me the power to be all You want me to be. Amen.

If you just prayed that prayer, share what you have done with someone—your wife, pastor, or a friend. I pray that you feel a fire burning in your life to count for God. God desires to build His kingdom in you and through you. Please commit yourself to *be* before you *do*. Then you will leave behind a legacy that has eternal value, for you will be His willing vessel to share the good news of Jesus Christ with the world around you.

> **The Bottom Line**
> - We must change paradigms in order to live in the second story.
> - If you present men with a great challenge, they will do something heroic.
> - God desires to build His kingdom in you and through you.

This week you discovered …
- the importance of knowing and loving God more deeply.
- knowing *who* you are is knowing *whose* you are.
- *Who* is your purpose is more important than *what* is your purpose.

What does God want you to do in response to this week's study?

_____

_____

Recite Colossians 3:1-3 as a closing thought for the week.

WEEK 5

DEFINING MOMENTS

Each day we make hundreds, even thousands, of decisions. We decide whether we will interrupt a staff meeting to take a phone call. We decide whether to make a follow-up phone call to find out if the prospect will buy or not.

There is another category of decision, however, that we might call a defining moment. Most men make two or three truly major decisions in the course of a year. Some of these major decisions are so significant that we might term them *defining moments*.

This week you will explore the questions associated with four defining moments in life.
- Control: To determine who's in charge.
- Character: To decide you will take the blows.
- Confidence: To accept God's love on God's terms.
- Calling: To discern and accept God's calling.

Some of these defining moments may have already happened in your life while others wait to be faced. Some answers are unfolding while others are still shrouded in mystery.

This week you will:
- Understand the implications and importance of defining moments;
- Discern where you are in each of four defining moments;
- Evaluate the next steps needed to move on in your walk with the Lord; and,
- Listen to the Lord's direction and voice as you make major decisions in your life.

WEEK 5, DEFINING MOMENTS

★ **DAY 1** ★
Defining Moments: What Are They?

★ **DAY 2** ★
Defining Moment 1: Control

★ **DAY 3** ★
Defining Moment 2: Character

★ **DAY 4** ★
Defining Moment 3: Confidence

★ **DAY 5** ★
Defining Moment 4: Calling

As you study, read the Scriptures, pray, and evaluate your life, ask for God's wisdom and guidance in your daily walk with Him.

Memorize and meditate daily on this text:

"Do not conform any longer to the patterns of this world, but be transformed by the renewing of your mind. Then you will be able to test and approve what God's will is–his good, pleasing and perfect will" (Romans 12:2).

It is my prayer that you will discern how God is shaping your life so that you will grow in confidence and will be obedient to your calling in Christ Jesus.

DAY 1

DEFINING MOMENTS: WHAT ARE THEY?

She taught the city's children of privilege in a wealthy, manicured neighborhood that stood in sharp contrast to an adjacent slum area. She kept to herself and tried not to venture out into neighboring areas.

One evening as she walked down the street, she heard a woman crying out for help. Just then a dying woman fell into her arms. Seeing that her condition was critical, she rushed her to the hospital. When the staff observed that the ill woman was poor, they were told to take a seat and wait. She sensed this woman was going to die without immediate medical attention, so she left and went to another hospital. Again, they were told to wait.

After the nurses and doctors still didn't come, she took the dying woman to her own home where, later that night, she died in the school teacher's arms.

This young teacher decided that would never happen again to anyone if she could help it. She decided to devote the rest of her life to easing the pain of those around her so they could live, or die, in dignity.

The city was Calcutta. The woman was Teresa. It was for her a defining moment.[1]

◆

Defining moments are monumental decisions that change the course or direction of a life.

Defining moments represent choices that may impact a life for many years, even a lifetime. They are defining moments because of their impact, because the consequences are so great, or because the wrong decision carries a high price tag. They are experiences, decisions, and choices we make at major junctions in life.

Scripture is filled with defining moments. Here are some people in the Bible who experienced defining moments. Read the following Scripture passages in your Bible, and describe in a word or phrase the defining moment for each person.

WEEK 5, DEFINING MOMENTS

Person	Text	Defining Moment
Abraham	Genesis 12:1-4	_____
Mary	Luke 1:26-38	_____
Peter	Matthew 16:13-16	_____
Paul	Acts 9:1-19	_____

Defining moments occur in different ways and for different reasons. God told Abraham to leave the security of his country and form a new nation. Mary was informed that she was chosen to give birth to Jesus. Peter proclaimed Jesus as the Christ, the Son of God. Paul was converted on the Damascus road. In each case, the person was faced with a defining moment that changed his or her life.

Sometimes men miss their defining moments. Following reelection, Nixon moved from the White House to Camp David for several weeks while putting together his new team. Harry Dent, special counsel to the president, was surprised to get the first call to Camp David. He boarded *Marine One* and made the short trip with Vice-President Spiro Agnew—the only person Nixon could not fire.

Harry Dent was further surprised when he was invited to meet privately with Nixon—even before Agnew. What was to be a brief meeting turned into a 2-hour session. Nixon wanted Dent to stay. Dent wanted to go home. After 10 minutes of discussion on that subject, Dent spent the rest of their time imploring the President to deal with Watergate and to consider his place in history. As he poured out his heart, he shook the President.[2]

Looking back, Harry Dent now realizes he missed his moment. For two hours he had the complete favor and attention of the President of the United States. Yet he chose to speak to the President about his place in history rather than his place in eternity. On the other hand, this incident became a powerful motivator for the rest of Harry Dent's life. Even a missed moment can become a defining moment.

THE SEASONS OF CRISIS AND RENEWAL

🖌 Describe a time you missed a defining moment. What was the result?

_____

_____

At other times men don't miss their defining moment—they simply choose to do wrong. You're tired, on the road, and she is available … The deal has unethical parts, but on the whole will make you a bundle of money … You usually are honest, but this is only a little white lie …

Remember Jonah? He had an opportunity to be used of God in a mighty way in Nineveh. Instead, he chose to run in the opposite direction. That decision in a defining moment put Jonah in the belly of a great fish (see Jonah 1).

David faced a defining moment when he saw Bathsheba bathing. He had a choice to make—to lust after her beauty or to look away. His decision led to adultery and the murder of Bathsheba's husband (see 2 Samuel 11). Everyone has defining moments. Some turn our lives toward God and others away from Him. Each negative defining moment in David's life brought him face-to-face with another defining moment—the decision of repentance and returning to God. David's failures didn't define his life. His decisions always to return to God defined David as a man "after the heart of God." Defining moments reveal a man's heart.

Here are some examples of milestones that may be defining moments for you.

- Getting married
- Going to college
- Joining a church
- Buying or selling a home
- Playing on a sports team
- Having children
- Taking a job
- Graduating from school
- Leading another person to Christ
- Confessing sin to another believer
- Following Jesus Christ as Lord and Savior
- Being sexually abstinent before marriage
- Being healed emotionally or physically by God
- Giving a significant gift to God or another person

WEEK 5, DEFINING MOMENTS

✎ Write down three important defining moments in your life and briefly describe what they revealed about your heart.

Defining Moment: **It Revealed:**

1._____   _____

2._____   _____

3._____   _____

This week we will explore the four types of defining moments that may have the *most* impact on our lives in a Season of Renewal.
1. Control: To determine who's in charge.
2. Character: To decide you will take the blows.
3. Confidence: To accept God's love on God's terms.
4. Calling: To discern and accept God's calling.

✎ As we proceed, ask yourself, "How would the Holy Spirit have me respond?" Pray, asking the Holy Spirit to guide you, teach you, and give you wisdom as you examine defining moments in your life.

The Bottom Line
- Defining moments are monumental decisions that change the course or direction of a life.
- They are defining moments because of their impact, because the consequences are so great, or because the wrong decision carries a high price tag.
- Sometimes men miss their defining moments; at other times men simply choose to do wrong.
- Defining moments reveal a man's heart.

---

[1]Anthony Robbins, *Awake the Giant Within* (New York: Simon and Schuster, 1991), 490.
[2]Harry S. Dent, *Cover Up* (San Bernadino: Here's Life Publishers, 1986), 33-34.

DAY 2

DEFINING MOMENT 1: CONTROL

I met a sharp young businessman on a plane. He prayed to receive Christ, but a few weeks later said, "I just can't give up control." Another man, a stockbroker, wouldn't attend our large Bible study, but wanted to meet privately. He had to be in charge—to do it his own way. Today he is divorced.

Every man must answer the question, "Who's in charge?" It is the issue of control. The Kingdom of God is not a prayer that instantly fixes everything. Loving God's Kingdom means turning from self to God, surrendering total control of one's life to Jesus Christ.

◆

The irony of surrender is that it leads not to defeat, but victory.

Here are some important Scriptures about control. Read each one and then identify what must be surrendered and who is to be in control.

Jesus said to his disciples, "If anyone would come after me, he must deny himself and take up his cross and follow me" (Matthew 16:24).
What's surrendered? _____
Who's to be in control? _____

"No one can serve two masters. Either he will hate the one and love the other, or he will be devoted to the one and despise the other. You cannot serve both God and Money" (Matthew 6:24).
What's surrendered? _____
Who's to be in control? _____

"I have been crucified with Christ and I no longer live, but Christ lives in me. The life I live in the body, I live by faith in the Son of God, who loved me and gave himself for me" (Galatians 2:20).
What's surrendered? _____
Who's to be in control? _____

WEEK 5, DEFINING MOMENTS

Obedience to God is the trademark of a Biblical Christian. It is how we demonstrate our love for God.

Jesus said, "Anyone who loves his father or mother more than me is not worthy of me; anyone who loves his son or daughter more than me is not worthy of me; and anyone who does not take his cross and follow me is not worthy of me. Whoever finds his life will lose it, and whoever loses his life for my sake will find it" (Matthew 10:37-39).

When we enter into fellowship with Jesus Christ, we surrender certain things. But we also receive things that are far greater than those we surrender. Match the first column with the correct answer in the second column. Scripture references provide the answers.

I Surrender...	From Jesus I Receive...
Death	• Power (2 Corinthians 12:9)
Blindness	• Forgiveness (1 John 1:9)
Grief	• Eternal life (John 3:16)
Weakness	• Joy (John 16:22)
Sin	• Sight (Luke 4:18)

If you have not made the decision to receive Christ as your Savior, every other decision you make will be different from what it would have been if you had. If you have salvation and know it, but wrestle against putting Christ in charge of your life, every decision you make will be at risk. Personally, I had been a follower of Christ for over 12 years before I settled once and for all who would be in charge of my life. It's a tough surrender to make.

The issue of control affects your future as well as your present. Do you make your own plans and then ask God to bless them? Do you try to control those around you—wife, children, employees, friends—and then ask God to fix any conflict that arises when they reject your control?

Here are some major areas of control that will bring you face-to-face with defining moments in your life. Who's in control in each area? Put an x on the bar to indicate where you are right now.

95

THE SEASONS OF CRISIS AND RENEWAL

Marriage (If you are married)

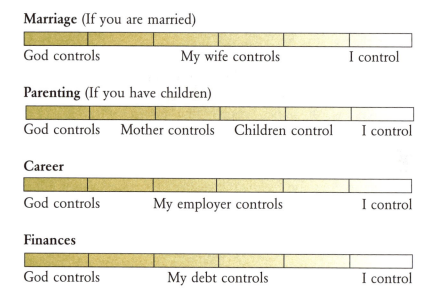

| God controls | My wife controls | I control |

Parenting (If you have children)

| God controls | Mother controls | Children control | I control |

Career

| God controls | My employer controls | I control |

Finances

| God controls | My debt controls | I control |

Have you settled the issue of who's in charge?

Here is the issue: Whether you know Christ or not, will you say to Jesus, "Take control of my life, make me the kind of man You want me to be"?

❏ Yes, I will.   ❏ No, I'm not ready to take that step.

If you are ready, ask God to take total control. Pray the above prayer (or one like it) surrendering all control to Him, and then begin to face specific areas of your life.

The Bottom Line
- Every man must answer the question, "Who's in charge?"
- The irony of surrender is that it leads not to defeat, but victory.
- Obedience to God is the trademark of a Biblical Christian.
- The issue of control affects your future as well as your present.

DAY 3

DEFINING MOMENT 2: CHARACTER

Todd was the president of his high-school class. He played first team on the basketball squad, and his dream was to play college ball.

After the Christmas break during Todd's senior year, the coach never played him again. No explanation was given. The Lord gave Todd the grace to sit on the bench. He never complained. He never even asked the coach why, though many parents of other players were asking.

Week after week, sitting in the stands, the father of another player gained a profound respect for Todd as he quietly observed Todd's character. Two years later this high-powered businessman needed a key executive assistant; his first call was to Todd. Today Todd attends college full-time and pays his tuition by working for this man part-time in a career field he loves.

Todd didn't get to play college basketball. The basketball scouts never saw him play. Yet, Todd did find a rewarding career field. That's because a different kind of "scout" saw the character with which he *didn't* play. In a way, Todd got a scholarship after all.

Every man must decide whether he will take the blows. This is the issue of suffering and hard times. Blows are defining moments. To suffer is to be in God's school.

◆

The hard blow is a hammer that shapes our character on God's anvil.

The apostle Paul describes God's way of producing character in us.

"Not only so, but we also rejoice in our sufferings, because we know that suffering produces perseverance; perseverance, character; and character, hope. And hope does not disappoint us, because God has poured out his love into our hearts by the Holy Spirit, whom he has given us" (Romans 5:3-5).

God uses difficulties, trials, and suffering as opportunities to shape and mold our character that we might be conformed to Jesus Christ.

THE SEASONS OF CRISIS AND RENEWAL

 Read each passage and discover what God is doing.

Passage	What Is God Doing In Us?
Consider it pure joy, my brothers, whenever you face trials of many kinds, because you know that the testing of your faith develops perseverance. Perseverance must finish its work so that you may be mature and complete, not lacking anything (James 1:2-4).	
In this you greatly rejoice, though now for a little while you may have had to suffer grief in all kinds of trials. These have come so that your faith … may be proved genuine and may result in praise, glory and honor when Jesus Christ is revealed (1 Peter 1:6-7).	
I want to know Christ and the power of his resurrection and the fellowship of sharing in his sufferings, becoming like him in his death, and so, somehow, to attain to the resurrection from the dead (Philippians 3:10-11).	

Suffering shapes character. We go through certain phases of character development.

Correction

Why do suffering, trials, and tests come our way? Sometimes God's agenda is correction. We suffer for doing *wrong*. We experience God's discipline as He lets us know that He loves us too much to let us have our own way.

God's discipline and correction are never punishment to hurt or damage us. Rather, His discipline in love turns us back to Him and His will for us. In fact, God's discipline strengthens us for the future.

God's discipline is described in Hebrews 12:5-11. Read the passage and underline any word or phrase that speaks directly to you.

> And you have forgotten that word of encouragement that addresses you as sons:
> "My son, do not make light of the Lord's discipline,
>   and do not lose heart when he rebukes you,
> because the Lord disciplines those he loves,
>   and he punishes everyone he accepts as a son."
> Endure hardship as discipline; God is treating you as sons. For what son is not disciplined by his father? If you are not disciplined (and everyone undergoes discipline), then you are illegitimate children and not true sons. Moreover, we have all had human fathers who disciplined us and we respected them for it. How much more should we submit to the Father of our spirits and live! Our fathers disciplined us for a little while as they thought best; but God disciplines us for our good, that we may share in his holiness. No discipline seems pleasant at the time, but painful. Later on, however, it produces a harvest of righteousness and peace for those who have been trained by it.

Persecution

While its true that sometimes we suffer for doing wrong, it is also true that sometimes we suffer for doing right. The Bible calls this *persecution*. God can still use that to shape our character. Suffering produces perseverance or endurance. It develops in us a resolve to remain committed to Jesus Christ no matter what the cost.

THE SEASONS OF CRISIS AND RENEWAL

🖌 How long have you been a Christian?
❏ Since _____. (date)   ❏ I'm not a Christian.

Which of the following terms would you use to describe your level of perseverance today?
   ❏ Stand firm   ❏ Shaky
   ❏ Waver   ❏ Fall apart

Have you grown in this area of your spiritual life since you first came to know Christ?
   ❏ Yes   ❏ No   ❏ Somewhat

According to Romans 5:3-5, suffering produces perseverance, and perseverance produces character. The Greek word for character means a tried, approved, and tested character. Having experienced both God's love in correction and faithfulness in persecution, we know we can stand firm on Jesus Christ. We have a foundation that cannot be shaken (see Matthew 7:24-27; Hebrews 12:28).

🖌 Describe a time in your life when your character was shaped significantly by God through correction or persecution.

_____

_____

_____

_____

Have you settled the issue of whether you will accept God's gracious blows? Will you stop chafing against the wisdom of God or complaining that you cannot go on? Get in touch with the Father, not in resignation, but in submission. This decision is a defining moment.

WEEK 5, DEFINING MOMENTS

What trial or correction are you experiencing? Write a prayer thanking God for what He is doing in you.

_____

_____

_____

_____

The Bottom Line
- The hard blow is a hammer that shapes our character on God's anvil.
- God uses difficulties, trials, and suffering as opportunities to shape and mold our character that we might be conformed to Jesus Christ.
- Suffering produces perseverance, character, and hope.
- While it is true that sometimes we suffer for doing wrong, it is also true that sometimes we suffer for doing right.

DAY 4

DEFINING MOMENT 3: CONFIDENCE

The Bible says eternal life is a free gift. You and I know there is no such thing as a free gift. Everything has a price. Right? So our response is to discount this news, though we long to believe it. We even take the action of placing our faith in Jesus, hoping it is true. Yet, a residue of doubt remains.

This is the issue of assurance of salvation, or eternal security. It is the problem of uncertainty about God's love, forgiveness, and salvation. *It can't be that easy,* we think. *There must be more to it.* Or we have faith, we believe, but we still feel we are not good enough or worthy. So we think, *I've been so bad. I need to do something to continue to earn God's favor.*

A typical way of dealing with this is to make a list of rules we can keep to try to be holy. This is salvation by *performance*.

🖌 Check the first two or three things you do to "recapture God's favor" after you sin.

- ❏ Go to church more
- ❏ Pray more earnestly
- ❏ Confess sin
- ❏ Be kind to my wife
- ❏ Read the Bible more
- ❏ Ask God's forgiveness immediately
- ❏ Accept God's grace and go on
- ❏ Spend more time doing good deeds

Another way of dealing with this is to constantly confess every slight offense we can think up: "Lord, forgive me for not smiling at that older woman in the grocery store yesterday." This is salvation by *confession*.

The problem with each of these is that we will always find there is one more thing to do or one more insignificant thing to confess. We can relax. Although eternal life is a free gift to us, it was not a free gift for Christ. He paid the price of the cross for our eternal life. All your past, present, and future sins have already been forgiven at the cross of Jesus Christ. Read this next sentence slowly:

◆

Everything that needs to be done for you to be good enough in God's sight has already been done by Jesus.

WEEK 5, DEFINING MOMENTS

Are you willing to accept this by faith, by trusting Jesus?

🖌 Following is a drawing of a cross. Write inside the cross your sins that have been paid for by Jesus. Then, mark through each sin as a reminder that Christ died for your sin, and He has promised that your true confession will bring forgiveness.

🖌 What does Scripture say about confidence and hope in Jesus? Read the following texts and discover your hope. Write about it.

Scripture	**My Hope**
"Do not let your hearts be troubled. Trust in God; trust also in me. In my Father's house are many rooms; if it were not so, I would have told you. I am going there to prepare a place for you. And if I go and prepare a place for you, I will come back and take you to be with me that you also may be where I am" (John 14:1-3).	_____ _____ _____ _____ _____ _____ _____ _____

THE SEASONS OF CRISIS AND RENEWAL

> Being confident of this, that he who
> began a good work in you will carry it on
> to completion until the day of Christ
> Jesus (Philippians 1:6).

Until we settle the issue of our eternal security, we will timidly perform and confess from a sense of duty. Our good deeds will lack the power of knowing that our salvation is true. Have you settled the issue of where you will spend eternity? Let the knowledge that God loves you move from your head to your heart. This issue is a defining moment.

 Where are you? Mark with an x where you are right now.

Uncertain of   Fully confident
eternal life   of eternal life

If you marked anywhere on the line other than the far right, it's time you settle this issue once and for all. The God who loves and saves you will never let you go! If you are uncertain, pray this simple prayer.

Lord Jesus, I receive you as my Lord and Savior. I confess my sins. I accept Your forgiveness and grace. Thank You for giving me eternal life through Your sacrifice on the cross—not through anything I have done or will do. Amen.

 Pray to God and express thanksgiving for your salvation and eternal life in Jesus Christ.

The Bottom Line
- Everything that needs to be done for you to be good enough in God's sight has already been done by Jesus.
- All your past, present, and future sins have already been forgiven at the cross of Jesus Christ.
- Until we settle the issue of our eternal security, we will timidly perform and confess from a sense of duty.

DAY 5

DEFINING MOMENT 4: CALLING

Nine out of ten men I spend time with have the same question on their minds: "What does God want me to do? What is His will for my life?"

As followers of Christ, we must commit ourselves to discern and accept God's calling. This is the issue of letting ourselves be equipped and sent wherever God wants.

◆

When God changes His calling on our lives, it is a defining moment.

An unsettled period often precedes a change in calling. Inevitably, God allows time between the calling and the sending to break down wrong thinking and actions, and to rebuild others.

The defining moment comes when we answer the question, "Am I going in Jesus' direction or my own?"

What keeps men from following Jesus' call? Check the barriers you have observed in other men's lives and circle those you have experienced.
- ☑ Pride
- ☑ Rebellion
- ❑ Persecution
- ❑ Apathy
- ❑ Social pressure
- ❑ Business interests
- ☑ Inability to hear God's voice
- ❑ Ignorance of God's Word
- ❑ Stigma associated with being a Christian
- ☑ Busyness
- ☑ Ambition
- ❑ Other: _____

Hearing God's voice is so important to responding to God's will for our lives. Jesus said, "I did tell you, but you do not believe. The miracles I do in my Father's name speak for me, but you do not believe because you are not my sheep. My sheep listen to my voice; I know them, and they follow me" (John 10:25-27).

Do you feel like you have a clear sense of God's calling on your life? Briefly describe your calling.

What practical step can you take to "hear God's voice" more clearly so that you can stay on track in your calling?

_____

_____

We cannot manufacture defining moments, but we should always have our antennae up for defining moments that come our way. I learned that from an acquaintance named John. He bumped into Marilyn at an eyeglasses store. He hadn't seen her for seven years, though their sons were good friends in school. The last time he saw her, she had cancer. From her emaciated appearance, John guessed she was still battling it. A month went by until one Saturday morning John woke up with Marilyn's phone number going through his head. He didn't call. He thought, *I'll call after church tomorrow.* After church the next day, his son encouraged him to call. He finally called, but the person who answered the phone said she had been taken to the hospital.

John was relieved. *It will be a lot easier to visit her in the hospital*, he thought. *Boy, am I a coward.* He procrastinated for another hour, then went to the store where he bought a bird-of-paradise flower, and headed for the hospital.

When he arrived at Marilyn's room, he noticed a stir. Her husband came out to greet him and said, "Thanks for coming, John. Marilyn died an hour ago."

Later, as John recalled this story, he said, "And then he hugged me. Like I deserved it or something. I feel like such a slug."

This event became a defining moment for John. Never again would he put off until later what he sensed the Lord wanted him to do now.

Personally, I write down defining moments and keep them in a file on my computer. Writing them down gives me a powerful reference tool to look at when I get confused about what I'm supposed to be doing. They provide benchmarks or signposts that I can look back on and refer to when God's call seems unclear.

WEEK 5, DEFINING MOMENTS

 What have you been putting off?

_____

When are you going to do it?

_____

Practice recording a defining moment in your life. Think of an experience or decision that turned you toward the Lord. Write it in detail on a separate sheet of paper.

> **The Bottom Line**
> - As followers of Christ we must commit ourselves to discern and accept God's calling.
> - When God changes His calling on our lives, it is a defining moment.
> - "Am I going in Jesus' direction or my own?"
> - We cannot manufacture defining moments, but we should always have our antennae up for defining moments that come our way.

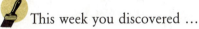 This week you discovered ...
- the importance of responding to defining moments.
- where you are in each of four defining moments.
- how to listen to the Lord's direction as you make major decisions.

What does God want you to do in response to this week's study?

_____

Recite Romans 5:3-4 as a closing thought for the week.

THE SEASON OF REFLECTION

REFLECTING ON THIS SEASON

1. The most important truth I learned for my spiritual life:
   _____
   _____

2. The Scripture passage that spoke to me with the most meaning (write the Scripture or your paraphrase of it):
   _____
   _____
   _____

3. One thing I need to confess to the Lord and ask forgiveness for:
   _____

4. One thing I need to praise the Lord for:
   _____

5. One important change the Lord and I need to make in my life:
   _____

6. The next step I need to take in obedience:
   _____

WEEK 6
REFLECTING ON CRISIS AND RENEWAL

As we have seen in the past five weeks, each man experiences crises when his world seems to be crashing in around him. And after these crises there is often a time of picking up the pieces, a time of renewal.

This week you will reflect on the process of working through crises that come your way. I have sought to summarize this week some of the important things God would say to you about your Seasons of Crisis and Renewal. Receive this as a word of encouragement as you walk through these seasons.

This week you will review:
- How to avoid burnout, or, if you have already hit the wall, to come out on the other side.
- The root problems that lead to a crisis, and how solving these problems can help us move out of our dark night into the light of God's new day.
- The typical pattern men go through that leads to restoration with God.
- How knowing and loving God should be the chief pursuit of every man's life.
- The nature, significance, and ways to handle defining moments in life.

As you review this material, open your heart and let the voice of the Father speak to you. Seek God's encouragement and instruction. Take time to examine your walk with God honestly and openly.

THE SEASONS OF CRISIS AND RENEWAL

As you study, pray, and reflect this week, keep in mind this verse:

"The thief [Satan] comes only to steal and kill and destroy; I [Jesus] have come that they might have life, and have it to the full" (John 10:10).

DAY 1

BURNOUT

During Week 1 of this study, you explored the issue of long-term burnout that can take place in a Season of Crisis. Today, let's review the main ideas from that week.

◆

**Day 1: Long-term burnout leaves men drained—
emotionally, physically, psychologically, and spiritually.**

Some crises come suddenly; others develop long-term. Some can be resolved quickly; others take a long time. And some problems, like the death of a child or visiting arrangements for children living with an ex-wife in another state, simply don't have solutions—we have to learn to live with them. This is a difficult reality to accept in an optimistic culture that often believes anything can be fixed given enough hard work.

One of the chief dangers we face in our fast-paced culture is long-term burnout.

🕯 On page 12 (week 1, day 1) you checked off symptoms of burnout that you experience regularly in your life. Look back over the list. Have you seen any changes during these last 5 weeks? What are they?

_____

_____

_____

Where are you? You may not be burned out, and that is good. On the other hand, you may be on the way, and you may know you are—or maybe you don't. Perhaps you have been through a meltdown before, or you may be in the middle of a burnout right now. One goal for this book is to help you avoid burnout or, if you have already hit the wall, to come out the other side. Because Somebody does care. Jesus cares.

◆

Day 2: All burnout comes as a result of a long series of poor decisions.

How does a man get burned out? Whether someone eats junk food or nutritious, healthy food, the difference is not immediately noticeable. In the same way, a season of crisis of burnout doesn't come suddenly. The crisis builds one day at a time, one choice at a time. These choices don't seem big at the moment, but when compounded and added to thousands of similar decisions, they inevitably lead to crisis.

Are you building your foundation on sand or rock? Building a balanced, rewarding life depends on making right choices about career, family, money, and God. We can, through self-examination, discover why we do what we do. We can look at the roots we have put down.

◆

Day 3: Poor choices about our values can lead to a crisis.

How do we start down the path toward long-term burnout? We lose direction when we buy into the values of our culture rather than the values of the kingdom.

Culture affects how we think, what we believe, and even the language we use to express ourselves. It is of paramount importance that we understand our culture.

You could say that we have a bad case of "isms,"—careerism, individualism, consumerism, materialism, relativism, and pluralism—which challenge us to win at all cost, to glory in self-reliance, to choose possessions over people, and to tolerate beliefs and behaviors with which we disagree. When we allow our values to be shaped by these forces, we are headed for long-term burnout.

On page 20, you listed four things that are important to you and also thought about any adjustments you needed to make. Does your life reflect the values of the kingdom? Have you made adjustments to you values to become more biblically based?

Day 4: All disappointment is a result of unmet expectations.

Unrealistic or unmet expectations can lead to a crisis. The problem we face is that our culture fosters high expectations, even rights. The siren song of our age is that "you can have it all"; moreover, you need it all to be truly happy.

The Bible teaches a different set of expectations. Romans 5:1-5 teaches that, if we've been justified by Christ through faith, then we can expect to have peace with God. We can expect to gain access to grace. And we can expect that God will enable us to live in a way that glorifies Him.

The Bible says, "Every good gift and every perfect gift is from above, and comes down from the Father of lights" (James 1:17 NKJV). Too often we don't show gratitude for the many blessings we do receive, and we become selfishly angered over the blessings we don't receive. Instead, we should receive everything with gratitude and humbly trust God when we don't get what we want.

Day 5: The purpose of our lives ought to be based on the quality of our character and conduct, not on the quantity of our circumstances over which we have no or limited control.

The best person to tell us the purpose of something is the person who created that thing. The One who knows the purpose of a man is the One who created man. Our purpose is grounded in whom we were created to be—not in what we think, plan, or advise.

Most of us get so busy with our own agenda that we have unresolved issues. Some unresolved issues relate to tasks, but by far the majority deal with relationships. We tend to take care of our tasks at the expense of our relationships. In the process, we can wound people and damage those we love the most.

Over time, making wrong choices in our values, expectations, purpose, and unresolved issues can lead to crises.

THE SEASONS OF CRISIS AND RENEWAL

🕯 Perhaps you realized that you are on the slippery slope that leads to crisis. How have you made changes in these areas during the last five weeks? What can you share with other men about your experience that can help them in these areas?

_____

_____

Throughout the study I have provided a summary of each day's material called "The Bottom Line." During these last five days, I want you to create your own "bottom line." What one truth has been most meaningful to you during each week of your study? At the end of each day this week, you will have an opportunity to write that truth. Reflect on what has been important to you. Ask God to help you live that truth each day.

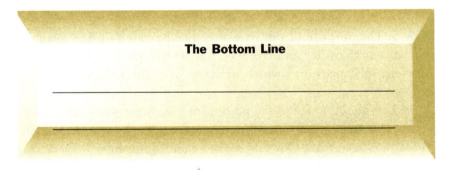

The Bottom Line

DAY 2
THE DARK NIGHT OF THE SOUL

The journey back to God often leads through crisis. Your Season of Crisis may be a dark night of the soul. During Week 2 of this study, we explored the root problems that can lead to a crisis, and how solving these problems can help move us out of our dark night into the light of God's new day. Let's review the main ideas of that week.

◆

Day 1: The turning point in our lives is when we stop seeking the God we want and start seeking the God who is.

There is a God we want, and there is a God who is. They are not the same God. God is who He is. No amount of wanting Him to be someone or something else will change anything. Our task is to be changed by God. To think we can outsmart God is pure tomfoolery.

A Biblical Christian accepts God's right to rule his life. But when a man is a Cultural Christian, he has divided his loyalties between God and the things of this world.

Before my own dark night of the soul, I remember hating my sin. But I also remember being powerless to overcome it. The dark night of the soul was God's gracious gesture to turn me back to him.

On page 32, you shaded a circle representing areas you are attempting to fully surrender to the Lord. How are you progressing?

◆

Day 2: Understanding Cultural Christianity is the first step to leaving it behind.

Like saltwater intrusion into a freshwater bay, Cultural Christianity pollutes Biblical Christianity slowly, with little observable notice. It is difficult to defeat an enemy you can't see and don't understand.

The problem with Cultural Christianity is twofold. First, many men never understand what the Bible says. They often have a respect for the Bible but no knowledge of its contents. The Bible presents a detailed picture of who we are, who God is, and how we should live in response.

Secondly, many men rebel against what they do know from the Bible and live by their own best thinking. Proverbs 14:12 declares, "There is a way that seems right to a man, but in the end it leads to death."

The self-help gospel is an example of this. It blends the human potential movement and selected Christian values. It suggests that self-esteem and success, not salvation, are the purpose of faith.

◆

Day 3: The object of the self-help gospel is to pursue the God we want. The object of the Gospel of the kingdom is to pursue the God who is.

The paradigms of Cultural Christianity and Biblical Christianity are opposite in almost every way. People who are caught up in Cultural Christianity need a whole new paradigm.

Sometimes, God allows us to pass through a time of crisis to help move us into this new paradigm. The first step that helps us come out on the other side of our time of crisis is accepting full responsibility for the problem.

To seek the God or gods we want is idolatry, and idolatry is sin. When we have sinned against God, we must express genuine remorse and then repent and pledge to act differently. There is a difference between worldly sorrow (merely feeling sorry for yourself) and godly sorrow: "Godly sorrow brings repentance that leads to salvation and leaves no regret, but worldly sorrow brings death" (2 Corinthians 7:10).

◆

Day 4: After assuming responsibility for the problem, we also must assume full responsibility for the solution.

An important part of moving out of a time of crisis is spiritual, physical, and emotional rest. We need to take responsibility to monitor gauges for each of these crucial areas of our lives. When we see the gauges moving toward "empty," we must also take responsibility to stop and refuel.

WEEK 6, REFLECTING ON CRISIS AND RENEWAL

🕯️ On pages 43 and 44, you noted some steps that you wanted to take to refuel in these three areas. Have you taken these steps? How have these things helped you during these last few weeks?

___

You must find God's solution to your problem and then implement it. I encourage you to set aside a block of time for physical rest, one for emotional rejuvenation, and one for spiritual renewal. The forgotten priority of our culture is rest, but rest is a priority with God.

◆

Day 5: There is no easy way out of a long-term crisis; it takes time to recharge and heal.

If you leave your car lights on overnight, your battery will run down. You can jump-start it and get it going, but the only way to bring the battery back permanently is to recharge it slowly.

God has anticipated your Season of Crisis and the dark night of your soul. God knows you need to be healed and restored in your relationship with Him and others.

🕯️ On pages 46 and 47, I suggested several Psalms that could help you in a time of crisis. Which of these passages spoke to your situation? What did God teach you that can help you make your way through your "dark night of the soul?"

___

The Bottom Line

DAY 3
RESTORATION

A Season of Crisis is often followed by a Season of Renewal. A man who abandons God will not be abandoned by God. One of the first steps in Renewal is restoration. During week 3 of this study, we looked at a typical pattern men go through that leads to restoration. Let's review the main ideas of that week.

◆

Day 1: Men who live by their own ideas end up in rebellion against God.

Many times this is not by a sinister plot, but by simple neglect of their relationship with their Heavenly Father. When men move away from their Father, their relationship begins to wane and diminish.

The story of the prodigal son shows how a man can suffer reversals because of his rebellion, then restoration through repentance. In the story we can detect four ways a man rebels against the Father: 1) Impatience with God's timing; 2) Desire to be in control; 3) Financial irresponsibility; 4) Moral lapse or decline.

On page 55, you prayed a prayer about these areas of your life. How has God changed you in these areas during the last few weeks?

_____

_____

_____

◆

Day 2: After a rebellious spirit has run its course, a reversal grabs our attention.

When all is going well, it's often hard for us to recognize our need for God. Jesus strongly warns the rich, not because riches are wrong, but be-

WEEK 6, REFLECTING ON CRISIS AND RENEWAL

cause the rich often become insensitive to their need for God and the needs of others. Then during a reversal, we sometimes focus on our circumstances rather than what God is doing. When our sins, like those of the prodigal son, blind us, we often turn to everyone but God.

Our response to reversals in life is critical. We have two choices. We can harden our hearts toward God, blaming Him and others for our problems; or, we can see reversals as an opportunity to throw ourselves completely on the mercies and resources of our loving Father.

◆

Day 3: Reversals will either lead you to run further from God or run from sin to God.

When the prodigal son found himself hungry and penniless in the pigpen, he was in a full-blown crisis. In the depths of his despair, this young man came to his senses and turned toward home.

A crisis is a gift from God that points us back toward Him. He does not let us destroy ourselves. The prodigal son repented and turned from his sin and back to his father. He saw the truth about his desperate situation, humbled himself, and headed home.

During this study, have you found that there are areas of your life where you are like the prodigal son? Briefly describe one area.

_____

_____

_____

Have you repented and returned to God? Briefly describe your experience.

_____

_____

_____

Day 4: When we return to God, He restores us and lavishes us with love.

When the prodigal son returned, his father had compassion on him. The father restored his son with great joy.

Restoration is not based on feelings. True confession and repentance always brings restoration with God. The price of this restoration is the shed blood of Jesus Christ. The more we consider the price Jesus paid for our sins, the more we desire to repent and come home to the Father.

Day 5: God comes running to meet us when we turn to Him in our hearts.

No sin is so terrible that God will not forgive you. No matter how far away from God you have been living, He can help you find your way back.

You can break out of the downward spiral into crisis at any point. A full-blown rebellion means crisis, but full-blown repentance means restoration.

If you have been suffering through a crisis of your own making and want to be reunited with your Heavenly Father, you can do so right now through prayer. Express your desire, your remorse for sinning against God, your sorrow for hurting those you love, your sense of unworthiness to even be called His son, and your pledge to change directions.

 The prodigal son went through four stages in his experience:

Rebellion ➔ Reversals ➔ Repentance ➔ Restoration

Has this paradigm helped your in evaluating your own relationship with God? Where have you seen this sequence in your life? Where are you now in the process?

_____

_____

WEEK 6, REFLECTING ON CRISIS AND RENEWAL

The Bottom Line

DAY 4
A NEW MESSAGE FOR MEN

Life is like a house with two stories. The first holds the lower order of man, earth, and created things. The second story contains God, heaven, and eternal things. God intends for men to live and move in both stories. We explored these ideas in week 4 of this study. Let's look back at the main ideas of that week.

◆

Day 1: The mainly economic man is not a whole man.

Many of us have believed the self-help gospel that teaches us to be good instead of sanctified. The goals of being a better husband and dad, managing time better, making better decisions, becoming a better money manager, and being successful are important, but they represent an anemic victory if we neglect the greater second-story demands of authentic faith.

There is no sustaining passion, no fire in the belly, of a man preoccupied with only the issues of the first story. Men get so busy that they don't have any time to consider their larger purpose. Also, in many cases the culture has influenced the church more than the church has influenced the culture.

God has a message for men stuck in the first story: "I love you, but you cannot be a Christian on your own terms." Trying to live a "good" life out of our own resources will always leave us drained and empty. God created us to find our richest fulfillment through a vibrant relationship with Him.

On page 71 and 72, you evaluated your participation in various "second-story" activities. Look back over your list. Have you made any changes in your priorities in recent days? Are you satisfied with your progress in these areas?

Day 2: The most important part of knowing who you are is knowing whose you are.

The question "Who am I?" deals with our earthly identity. The question "Whose am I?" deals with our identity in relation to our Creator. To know ourselves, we must also know something of the nature and character of the One who made us and His design, plan, and purpose for mankind.

Day 3: We cannot answer the question "What is the purpose of my life?" until we answer the question "Who is the purpose for my life?"

The point is simple, yet profound. God created us to be human "beings", not human "doings." Serving Jesus Christ is important–it's just not the most important thing. Serving God is best when it comes from gratitude for knowing God.

Most men would prefer to do something for God rather than simply be with Him. But a task-oriented approach to Christian faith can lead to a huge spiritual defeat.

If we don't grasp who is the purpose of our lives, what we do won't have much meaning. What a joy it is to serve Jesus because we first worship Him, love Him, commune with Him, and hear His voice!

Day 4: Knowing and loving God should be the chief pursuit of every man's life.

The key to staying on track is a life of devotion and study of God. Then, after a man is filled up to the overflow with Jesus, he should do whatever it is he is called to do–practice law or medicine, fix plumbing, sell, manage, mow lawns, drive a truck, or do whatever.

A life of devotion means to love God more and more. We were made to have a vibrant relationship with God. When we love God at the core of our being, He gives us a sense of meaning that overflows into every area of our lives.

THE SEASONS OF CRISIS AND RENEWAL

A life of study means to know God more and more. The more clearly we know God, the more clearly we know who we should be. The brilliance of His character evaporates the fog that blankets our minds.

🕯️ A man's relationship with God must always be a higher priority that the work he does for God. Have you seen growth in recent days in your relationship with God? How have you specifically learned to love God more?

Write down one specific thing you have learned or re-learned about God that has impacted you during this study.

◆

Day 5: We must change paradigms in order to live in the second story.

If you present men with a great challenge, the will do something heroic. Most men want to be "all the way" Christians, not "statistical" Christians. They simply need someone to show them how.

I pray that you feel a fire burning in your life to count for God. Please commit to be before you do. Then you will leave behind a legacy that has eternal value, for you will be a willing vessel to share the good news of Jesus Christ with the world around you.

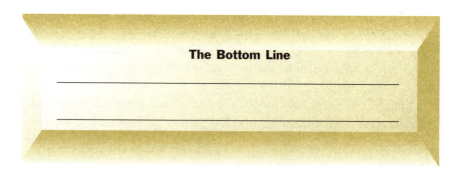

The Bottom Line

DAY 5
DEFINING MOMENTS

Each day we make hundreds, even thousands of decisions. However, most men make only two or three truly major decisions in the course of a year. Some of these major decisions are so significant that we might call them defining moments. Let's consider again the most important ideas to remember about defining moments.

◆

Day 1: Defining moments are monumental decisions that change the course or direction of a life.

Defining moments are choices that may impact a life for many years, even a lifetime. They are experiences, decisions, and choices we make at major junctions in life.

Sometimes men miss defining moments. Other times, they simply choose to do wrong. Defining moments reveal a man's heart.

◆

Day 2: The irony of surrender is that it leads not to defeat, but victory.

Every man must answer the issue of "Who's in charge?" It is the issue of control. Loving God means turning from self to God, surrendering total control of one's life to Jesus Christ.

The issue of control effects your future as well as your present. Every decision you make is influenced by who you believe is really in charge of your life.

◆

Day 3: The hard blow is a hammer that shapes our character on God's anvil.

To suffer is to be in God's school. Every man must decide whether he will take the blows. Blows from God are defining moments.

Sometimes God sends suffering, trials, and tests into our lives to correct us. At other times, we may be persecuted for doing right. God can still use this to shape our character. Suffering produces perseverance, character, and hope (Romans 5:3-5).

◆

Day 4: Everything that needs to be done for you to be good enough in God's sight has already been done by Jesus.

Many men face uncertainty about God's love, forgiveness, and salvation. A typical way to deal with this is to make a list of rules we can keep to try to be holy. This is salvation by performance.

We can relax. Jesus is the one who earned God's favor for us. All your past, present, and future sins have already been forgiven at the cross of Jesus Christ.

Until we settle the issue of our confidence in Christ, we will timidly perform and confess from a sense of duty. Our good deeds will lack the power that comes from the assurance of our salvation.

◆

Day 5: When God changes his calling in our lives, it is a defining moment.

As followers of Christ, we must commit ourselves to discern and accept God's calling. The defining moment comes when we answer the question, "Am I going in Jesus' direction or my own?"

While we cannot manufacture defining moments, we should always have our antennae up for defining moments that come our way. Taking the time to stop and think through our defining moments can help us gain clarity and certainty about God's calling on our lives.

We have described four types of defining moments: Control, Character, Confidence, and Calling. Place an x on the following bars to indicate where you think you are in each of these areas.

I control my life			I am fully surrendering to Christ		

I seek to avoid suffering at all costs.			I allow God to shape my character through suffering		

WEEK 6, REFLECTING ON CRISIS AND RENEWAL

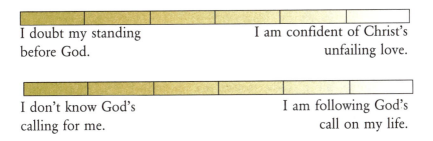

I doubt my standing before God. / I am confident of Christ's unfailing love.

I don't know God's calling for me. / I am following God's call on my life.

Pray a prayer thanking God for the way He has worked in your life during this study. Ask Him to continue His work in you in the weeks and months ahead.

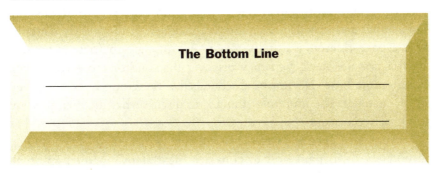

The Bottom Line

What now? If you have not studied the other books in *The Seven Seasons of a Man's Life* collection, I encourage you to do so. The back cover of this book provides information to guide you in your selection.

As you turn now to that unique set of problems and opportunities that only you face, know you are not alone, for God makes the seasons.

LEADER GUIDE

In the next six weeks, you will be exploring *The Seasons of Crisis and Renewal* with a group of men. This leader guide is appropriate for home groups, men's Bible study groups, accountability groups, discipleship and prayer groups, and one-to-one discipling.

The Introductory Session is 90 minutes; weekly sessions are 50 minutes. Consider these suggestions for each session.

Opening Time–This can be a time of sharing and getting caught up on what's happened during the week. Each session has a suggested exercise for this opening time.

Study and Sharing Time–Key exercises and questions for discussion and sharing are provided. Exercises are taken from the weekly material with a page reference usually given. As your group focuses on the material for the week, you may discover that one or more issues will require more time. Do not be discouraged if the group does not cover all the material. The important thing is to discuss what the men in your group *need* to discuss.

Prayer and Closing Time–This is a time for men to pray together corporately or in pairs and to consider "next steps" in their spiritual walks with the Lord.

Each session needs a facilitator; it may be the same person or a different person for each session.

Before each group session the facilitator should:
- Pray for each group member.
- Complete all daily studies for that week.
- Encourage members to complete their work.
- Make handouts of the session material for those who want a separate copy, who forget their book, or who are new to the group.
- Contact members who were absent the last session.

Before the *first* group session, the facilitator should complete Week 1 of the material so he can speak from experience on how he set aside time daily to study.

Introductory Session

The first group session of *The Seasons of Crisis and Renewal* is a time of distributing the book, reviewing the material, and understanding the format for the group sessions. This session includes a 45-minute video presentation by Patrick Morley. Each man should have a copy of the listening sheet provided in the video guide.

During the Session

1. Each man introduces himself and takes one minute to tell about himself and his family. (15 minutes)
2. Each man shares one expectation he has of the group and why he came to the group. (10 minutes)
3. Show the video featuring Patrick Morley's challenge and overview of *The Seasons of Crisis and Renewal*. (45 minutes)
4. Give each man a copy of the book. Explain that a commitment needs to be made to read the daily study and fill in all the exercises. Each daily study will take 20 to 30 minutes. (5 minutes)
5. As a group, look at Week 1, Day 1. Have everyone glance over the material and ask any questions they may have about how to use it. (5 minutes)
6. Ask for prayer requests. Repeat the prayer requests, and pray that God's Spirit will guide each man as he studies during the coming week. (7 minutes)
7. Remind each man to complete Week 1 before the next session and to bring his book to every group session. Announce the day, time, and place for the next session. (3 minutes)

Session 1: Burnout

Before the Session

- Each man should have completed Week 1.
- This week's facilitator should make copies of this sheet for anyone who wants an extra copy, who may forget his book, or who is new to the group.
- Pray for each person in the group and for the session, asking for God's wisdom and guidance.

During the Session

Opening Time (5-7 minutes)

1. Greet each other as you arrive.
2. Go around the group with each man sharing:
   - One way God blessed me last week was…
   - My greatest lesson from God last week was…

Study and Sharing Time (35-40 minutes)

3. We all face times in our lives when we "hit the wall" and have the "urge to quit." Share with a partner what kinds of crises precipitate a feeling of hitting the wall or the urge to quit in your life. After each man has shared, pause and pray for each other.

6. With a partner, answer the following questions about **expectations**.
   - What do you expect of yourself?
   - What are your wife's expectations of you?
   - What are your children's expectations of you?
   - What are the expectations of your employer for you? If you are self-employed, what expectations do you have for yourself in your work?

   Evaluate these expectations. Are they realistic or will your expectations set you up to fail?

7. When you fail to meet an expectation of your own or of someone else, how do you feel? Share you response with your partner.

8. How we understand our **purpose** in life dramatically affects us and others. Not having a purpose or having the wrong purpose for life will bring us into a season of crisis. With a partner, share:

   My God-given purpose in life is _____.

9. **Unresolved issues** focus our attention on problems instead of purpose. Share with a partner any unresolved issues you have determined you are going to resolve because of this week's study.

- What are some of the most common symptoms of burnout you see in men around you?
- When you notice these symptoms in your own life, what steps do you take to cure them?

5. A crisis results from repeatedly making poor choices about values, expectations, purpose, and unresolved issues. What are the basic assumptions, the bedrock **values** and **beliefs** that govern your life? Complete each sentence below that reflects your basic beliefs. I believe that...

God is _____
Jesus is _____
The Holy Spirit is _____
Family is _____
Sin is _____
Eternal life is _____
The most important thing in life is _____
Love is _____
Salvation is _____

Share with the entire group one value from your list and briefly explain why it is important in your life.

them as a total group.

- Long-term burnout leaves men drained emotionally, physically, psychologically, and spiritually.
- All burnout is the result of a long series of poor decisions.
- Poor choices about our values can lead to a crisis.
- All disappointment is a result of unmet expectations.
- The purpose of our lives ought to be based on the *quality* of our *character* and *conduct*, not on the *quantity* of our *circumstances* over which we have no or limited control.

Prayer and Closing Time (5 minutes)

11. If you are in danger of suffering burnout, ask a partner to pray with you. Pray that God would give you the strength to make needed changes in your life.

If you have been through burnout in the past, ask God to help you remember the lessons you learned through that experience.

6. The first step in turning around a season of crisis is to assume full responsibility for the problem. The second step is to assume full responsibility for the solution. That involves keeping our "tanks" full. With a partner, discuss the level of your spiritual, physical, and emotional tank. Share with each other practical ideas you've found for raising the level of any that are low.

7. Listed below are the BIG IDEAS for the week. Review them as a total group.

- The turning point of our lives is when we stop seeking the God we want and start seeking the God who is.
- Understanding Cultural Christianity is the first step to leaving it behind.
- The object of the self-help gospel is to pursue the God we want. The object of the gospel of the Kingdom is to pursue the God who is.
- After assuming responsibility for the problem, we must assume full responsibility for the solution.
- There is no easy way out of a long-term crisis; it takes time to recharge and heal.

❋ Session 2: The Dark Night of the Soul

Before the Session

- Each man should have completed Week 2.
- This week's facilitator should make copies of this sheet for anyone who wants an extra copy, who may forget his book, or who is new to the group.
- Pray for each person in the group and for the session, asking for God's wisdom and guidance.

During the Session

Opening Time (5-7 minutes)

1. Greet each other as you arrive.
2. Go around the group with each man sharing:
   - One way God blessed me last week was…
   - My greatest lesson from God last week was…

Study and Sharing Time (35-40 minutes)

3. Here is a great problem: Men become Cultural Christians when they are not Biblical Christians. Define below the terms Cultural Christianity and Biblical Christianity

Discuss with the men in your group the characteristics of each one.

4. A man desiring to pass from Cultural Christianity to Biblical Christianity often passes through "the dark night of the soul." This is not a time of punishment but rather a time of testing and spiritual growth.

With a partner, tell about a wilderness experience you have had and what you learned about God's grace.

5. Cultural Christians are self-made men led by a self-help gospel.

As a total group discuss:
- Where do you see evidences of the self-help gospel in your life, church, and culture?
- Which self-help theme influences you most?
- What does the Bible teach about the self-help gospel? Ask three men to read Psalm 20:7; Proverbs 16:1-3; and Proverbs 19:21.

8. With a partner, pray a prayer like the following:

Almighty God, thank You for being with us during our dark night of the soul. We want to learn every lesson you have for us during this time. Holy Spirit, guide us through the night and draw us back into the light of fellowship with the God who is. In Jesus' Name, Amen.

Session 3: Restoration

Before the Session

- Each man should have completed Week 3.
- This week's facilitator should make copies of this sheet for anyone who wants an extra copy, who may forget his book, or who is new to the group.
- Pray for each person in the group and for the session, asking for God's wisdom and guidance.

During the Session

Opening Time (5-7 minutes)

1. Greet each other as you arrive.
2. Go around the group with each man sharing:
   - The most important thing I learned from the parable of the prodigal son this week was …
   - In looking at my life and the stages of the prodigal son's life, right now I am in the stage of … (rebellion, reversals, repentance, restoration)

Study and Sharing Time (35-40 minutes)

3. Think back over the months or years that you have known Jesus Christ as Lord and Savior. Share briefly with three other men events or experiences in which you found

---

6. The study this week was based on the prodigal son. Have someone read Luke 15:11-24. What did the father do to **restore** his son? Discuss your answer with the entire group.

7. With a partner, share anything that keeps you from reaching out to God for restoration and forgiveness.

8. Listed below are the BIG IDEAS for the week. Review them as a group.

- Men who live by their own ideas end up in rebellion against God.
- After a rebellious spirit has run its course, a reversal grabs our attention.
- Reversals will either lead you to run further *from* God or run from sin *to* God.
- When we return to God, He restores us and lavishes us with love.
- God comes running to meet us when we turn to Him in our hearts.

Refer to the exercise on pages 52-53 if needed.

4. With the same three men, discuss the following questions.
   - When you find yourself in a cycle of **rebellion**, what keeps you from turning back to the loving Father and asking forgiveness? (See page 57.)
     - ☐ My pride.
     - ☐ My belief that I can turn things around by myself.
     - ☐ My depression keeps me from doing anything.
     - ☐ My desire to show God I'm in control.
     - ☐ My self-deceit that I'm really OK when I'm not.
     - ☐ Other: _____.
   - Have you ever been through a period of reversals, gone to your friends for help, but no one would lend a hand? Describe that time.

5. **Repentance** means _____.
   As a total group discuss why it is so difficult for men to turn from sin to God.

9. The pattern you studied this week is repeated throughout life:

   Rebellion ➤ Reversals ➤ Repentance ➤ Restoration

   A full-blown rebellion means crisis, but full-blown repentance means restoration. Immediate repentance brings immediate forgiveness. You may reap the consequences of your sin for some time to come. But God will restore, love, and forgive you. Close by having someone read Psalm 103:11-12 (page 67) and leading the group in prayer.

5. Examine where you are right now in your relationship with Christ. Circle one phrase on each line that represents where your relationship with Jesus is at this moment.

Focused on tasks	or	Focused on Christ
Listening to others	or	Listening to Christ
Seeking a purpose	or	Seeking Christ
Wondering who I am	or	Knowing Whose I Am

Share with two other men why you circled the phrases you circled.

6. Listed below are the BIG IDEAS for the week. Review them as a total group.

- The mainly economic man is not a whole man.
- The most important part of knowing *who* you are is knowing *whose* you are.
- We cannot answer the question "*What* is the purpose of my life?" until we answer the question "*Who* is the purpose of my life?"

Session 4: A New Message for Men

Before the Session

- Each man should have completed Week 4.
- This week's facilitator should make copies of this sheet for anyone who wants an extra copy, who may forget his book, or who is new to the group.
- Pray for each person in the group and for the session, asking for God's wisdom and guidance.

During the Session

Opening Time (5-7 minutes)

1. As men arrive, have each man share: The most significant divine thing that happened in my life this week was…

Study and Sharing Time (35-40 minutes)

2. Francis Schaeffer wrote that life consists of a first story and a second story. The first story holds the lower order of man, earth, and created things. The second story contains God, heaven, and eternal things. God intends for the new man in Jesus Christ to live and move in both stories. Read Colossians 3:1-3 and 1 Corinthians 7:31 (page 69).

principle of *whose we are* versus *who we are*. Jesus describes His relationship with the Father throughout the Gospel of John. One such description is found in John 8:28-29: "When you have lifted up the Son of Man, then you will know that I am the one I claim to be and that I do nothing on my own but speak just what the Father has taught me. The one who sent me is with me; he has not left me alone, for I always do what pleases Him."

Underline everything that Jesus says which points to His relationship with His Father.

As a total group look at this passage and discuss:

- Why was Jesus so confident in His relationship to God?
- How did His relationship with God give Jesus power to face crises in His life?

4. We are *who* we are because of *whose* we are. Have someone read John 15:5: "I am the vine; you are the branches. If a man remains in me and I in him, he will bear much fruit; apart from me you can do nothing." How does this passage link our identity and purpose to Christ?

- Knowing and loving God should be the chief pursuit of every man's life.
- We must change paradigms in order to live in the second story.

Prayer and Closing Time (5 minutes)

7. An organizing principle for our lives could be:

To commit ourselves to a life of devotion and study of God, then "doing" what God has called us to do.

As a total group, invite each man to share how this principle could have a practical impact on his life. Pray the Lord's Prayer in unison to close the session.

Session 5: Defining Moments

Before the Session

- Each man should have completed Week 5.
- This week's facilitator should make copies of this sheet for anyone who wants an extra copy, who may forget his book, or who is new to the group.
- Pray for each person in the group and for the session, asking for God's wisdom and guidance.

During the Session

Opening Time (5-7 minutes)

1. As the men arrive, have each man share the greatest decision he has ever made, one that changed the direction and course of his life.

Study and Sharing Time (35-40 minutes)

2. Divide into four groups. Each group choose one of the four defining moments discussed this past week. Each group determine from the book and personal experiences what the key question is in the defining moment assigned to them. If the group is small, assign two defining moments to each group.

Marriage (If you are married)

God controls — My wife controls — I control

Parenting

God controls — Mother controls — Children control — I control

Career

God controls — My employer controls — I control

Finances

God controls — My debt controls — I control

With a partner, discuss two areas that concern you.

6. Ask for volunteers to share when they experienced one of the four defining moments: control, character, confidence, calling. Ask, "What was your defining moment? What was your response? What have been the consequences in your

- Control: To determine who's in charge.
- Character: To decide you will take the blows.
- Confidence: To accept God's love on God's terms.
- Calling: To discern and accept God's calling.

3. In the small groups, have each man share an experience from one of the defining moments in his life.

4. In the total group, ask each man to share which of the following biblical persons they identify most with and why (see page 91). Have someone summarize the passage and another person identify the defining moment.

Person	Text	Defining Moment
Abraham	Genesis 12:1-4	
Mary	Luke 1:26-38	
Peter	Matthew 16:13-16	
Paul	Acts 9:1-19	

5. Let's focus on one type of defining moment–control. Who's in control in each of the following areas? Put an x on the bar to indicate where you are right now.

them as a total group.

- Defining moments are monumental decisions that change the course or direction of a life.
- The irony of surrender is that it leads not to defeat, but victory.
- The hard blow is a hammer that shapes our character on God's anvil.
- Everything that needs to be done for you to be good enough in God's sight has already been done by Jesus.
- When God changes His calling on our lives, it is a defining moment.

Prayer and Closing Time (5 minutes)

In groups of two or three, have each man ask the others to pray for him to grow in surrendering control to the Lord.

Session 6: Reflecting on Crisis and Renewal

Before the Session

- Each man should have completed Week 6.
- This week's facilitator should make copies of this sheet for anyone who wants an extra copy, who may forget his book, or who is new to the group.
- Pray for each person in the group and for the session, asking for God's wisdom and guidance.
- Have three-by-five-inch cards available for each man in the group.

During the Session

Opening Time (5-7 minutes)

1. Greet each other as you arrive. Give each man a three-by-five-inch card. Have each man write his personal definition of success on the card. Be creative. Someone collect the cards and shuffle them. Read the definitions and let everyone try to guess who wrote each one.

3. As a total group, answer the following questions that are based on the main points of this week's review:
  - How do you avoid burnout, or, if you have already hit the wall, how do you come out on the other side?
  - What are the root problems that lead to a crisis, and how does solving these problems can help us move out of our dark night into the light of God's new day?
  - What is the typical pattern men go through that leads to restoration with God?
  - How do you personally know and love God?
  - How do you handle defining moments in your life.

4. With three other men, answer each of the following questions. Give everyone an opportunity to share.
  - Who and what is the enemy?
  - What is my central flaw?
  - What do I look forward to in eternity?

Prayer and Closing Time (5 minutes)

5. Acknowledge the value of each man that has participated in the group. Discuss plans for studying another book in this collection or following up on anything left undone in this study.

2. Read the following Scripture in unison. Discuss how you might change your definitions of success based on this text.

> Blessed is the man
>   who does not walk in the
>   counsel of the wicked
> or stand in the way of sinners
>   or sit in the seat of mockers.
> But his delight is in the law of the Lord,
>   and on his law he meditates day and night.
> He is like a tree planted by streams of water,
>   which yields its fruit in season
>   and whose leaf does not wither.
>   Whatever he does prospers.
> Not so the wicked!
>   They are like chaff that the wind blows away.
> Therefore the wicked will not stand in
>   the judgment,
>   nor sinners in the assembly of the righteous.
> For the Lord watches over the way
>   of the righteous,
>   but the way of the wicked will perish (Psalm 1).

below. Commit to one another to pray over the list in the coming weeks and to check up on one another. Close the study with prayer.

Group Prayer List

Names	Prayer Requests
_____	_____
_____	_____
_____	_____
_____	_____
_____	_____
_____	_____

CHRISTIAN GROWTH STUDY PLAN

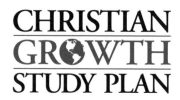

In the **Christian Growth Study Plan (formerly Church Study Course),** this book *The Seven Seasons of a Man's Life: The Seasons of Crisis and Renewal* is a resource for course credit in the subject area Personal Life of the Christian Growth category of diploma plans. To receive credit, read the book, complete the learning activities, show your work to your pastor, a staff member or church leader, then complete the following information. This page may be duplicated. Send the completed page to:

Christian Growth Study Plan
One LifeWay Plaza
Nashville, TN 37234-0117
FAX: (615)251-5067
Email: *cgspnet@lifeway.com*

For information about the Christian Growth Study Plan, refer to the Christian Growth Study Plan Catalog. It is located online at *www.lifeway.com/cgsp*. If you do not have access to the Internet, contact the Christian Growth Study Plan office (1.800.968.5519) for the specific plan you need for your ministry.

The Seven Seasons of a Man's Life: The Seasons of Crisis and Renewal
CG-0179

PARTICIPANT INFORMATION

Social Security Number (USA ONLY-optional) | Personal CGSP Number* | Date of Birth (MONTH, DAY, YEAR)

Name (First, Middle, Last) | Home Phone

Address (Street, Route, or P.O. Box) | City, State, or Province | Zip/Postal Code

Email Address for CGSP use

Please check appropriate box: ☐ Resource purchased by church ☐ Resource purchased by self ☐ Other

CHURCH INFORMATION

Church Name

Address (Street, Route, or P.O. Box) | City, State, or Province | Zip/Postal Code

CHANGE REQUEST ONLY

☐ Former Name

☐ Former Address | City, State, or Province | Zip/Postal Code

☐ Former Church | City, State, or Province | Zip/Postal Code

Signature of Pastor, Conference Leader, or Other Church Leader | Date

*New participants are requested but not required to give SS# and date of birth. Existing participants, please give CGSP# when using SS# for the first time. Thereafter, only one ID# is required. **Mail to:** Christian Growth Study Plan, One LifeWay Plaza, Nashville, TN 37234-0117. Fax: (615)251-5067.

Revised 4-05